theme
gardens

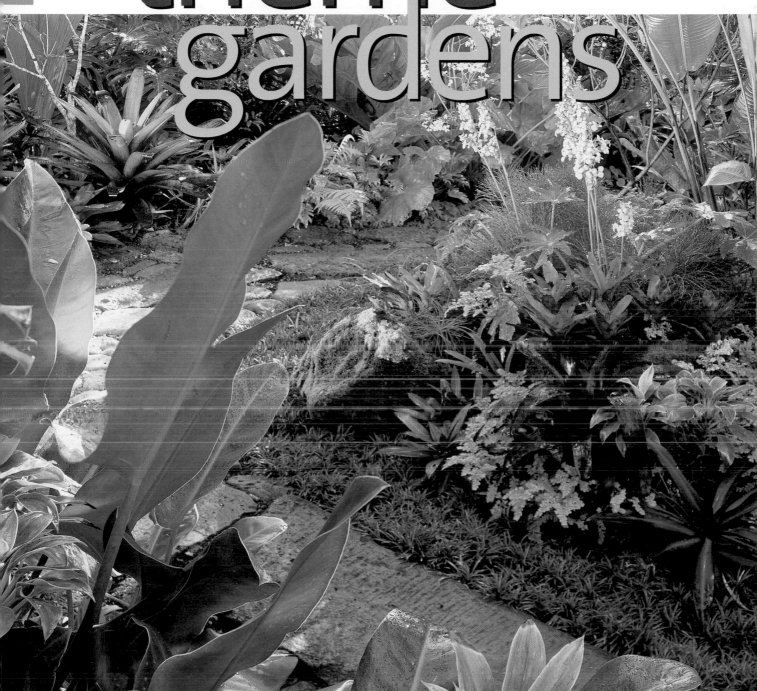

by Hazel White, Janet H. Sanchez, and the Editors of Sunset Books

SUNSET PUBLISHING CORP. | MENLO PARK, CALIFORNIA

In with the New

Gardens change. Of course, the plants grow, and some are crowded out while others extend their leaves in wide-spreading canopies. But gardens also change because we delight in change. We enjoy trying new plants, new colors, new materials, new projects. Often, the grass seems so much greener on the other side that we decide we want an entirely fresh garden—Mediterranean instead of the natural style we chose before, or tropical to make sense of all the orchids we've acquired, or formal because we've come to appreciate the simplicity of sunlight traveling over a fine-textured clipped hedge.

This book introduces you to the essential features of eight distinctive themes, including what you might use as a starting point and how to make a transition from one theme to another. You'll also find lots of easy and enjoyable projects, to help you implement each theme effectively, and suggestions for perfect plant choices.

Turn to the theme that interests you most, or start at the beginning chapter, "Deciding on a Theme," to learn about options for yards of different sizes and tricks for making multiple themes work in your garden.

SUNSET BOOKS
Vice President and General Manager:
  Richard A. Smeby
Vice President and Editorial Director:
  Bob Doyle
Production Director: Lory Day
Operations Director: Rosann Sutherland
Retail Sales Development Manager:
  Linda Barker
Executive Editor: Bridget Biscotti Bradley
Art Director: Vasken Guiragossian

STAFF FOR THIS BOOK:
Managing Editor and Copy Editor:
  Zipporah W. Collins
Sunset Books Senior Editor, Gardening:
  Marianne Lipanovich
Writers: Hazel White, Janet H. Sanchez
Designer: David Bullen
Illustrator: Erin O'Toole
Photography Editor: Cynthia Del Fava
Prepress Coordinator: Eligio Hernandez
Proofreaders: Desne Ahlers, Tom Hassett
Indexer: Ron Strauss

Cover design: Vasken Guiragossian,
  David Bullen
Cover photographs:
  top, Jerry Harpur
  bottom left, Roger Foley
  bottom middle, C. Nichols/M.A.P.
  bottom right, Dency Kane

10 9 8 7 6 5 4 3 2
First printing January 2004

Library of Congress Control Number 2003109781. ISBN 0-376-03303-7.

Printed in the United States.

For additional copies of *Theme Gardens* or any other Sunset Book, call 1-800-526-5111 or visit us at www.sunsetbooks.com.

Contents

Deciding on a Theme

A THEME GARDEN IS FUN—fun to make and fun to visit. It's a magical place you can pull together by ensuring that your tree, shrubs, chair, and ornaments work to a single effect. It's a cure for muddle and mishmash. Because of that, it's refreshing and inviting.

A theme garden creates an illusion of sorts, and visitors to the garden become part of it, like characters in a play. For example, think whether walking up a formal path flanked with clipped yew doesn't make you want to stand more erect or button your jacket or straighten your tie and whether finding yourself on a porch listening to a fountain and surrounded by lacy Japanese maples doesn't make you want to sink down in the wicker chair and live in this sweet place all your life.

Theme gardens are effective gardens. They have an essence, a combination of elements that most vividly produces the effect. This book presents those essences, so you can get going quickly from scratch or confidently rearrange your garden in a way that makes more sense.

Personality Test

What's your style? Do you like quiet, green, secret gardens where you can rest, or do you prefer gardens for entertaining that bowl guests over with stimulating color and pattern? Do you collect objects and plants galore, or do you prefer clean lines and no clutter? Flip through this book to see what theme takes your fancy. Let your eyes do the work; listen for thoughts that begin "I've always wanted . . ." or "I wish I could . . ."

Give full rein to daydreaming, but, before you begin actually shopping for a theme garden, check your plans against your personal gardening history. Do you have one lifelong interest in a particular kind of garden, or do your desires change with gardening fashions? Do you like to spend most of your time in the garden relaxing, or working? The answers to these questions might determine whether you do a complete garden makeover to one theme or set up your garden so that you can experiment as and when you please.

Having It All

Don't be alarmed if you want many of the themes in this book; you can have them if you have some space—less space than you probably think (see the following pages). If you can't have them all at one time, there's a way to organize a garden for an easy change of theme.

Consider building the foundations of your garden in a neutral style, the equivalent of painting your indoor rooms white. Make it predominantly green, keep the paving simple, and leave lots of room for container plantings. Then on that neutral stage mount performances that run for as long as your enthusiasms last. When you're done, you can change the pots and just a few other elements to pull off the next piece of magic.

A garden can often be easily dressed up with a new theme. If the owners of the bottle bank (left) tire of the bottles, they can replace them with rosemaries for a Mediterranean theme or ferns for a Japanese or natural theme. If the pot in the simple Zen space below is needed somewhere else in Anne Hirondelle's yard in Port Townsend, Washington, a small formal pool or a Ping-Pong table could take its place. Design, left: Bob Clark.

One Theme or Many Themes

A Single Theme

A single theme is a choice for a coherent world that starts from the house doors and runs to the garden boundaries. Each way a visitor turns through the garden another view of this world is revealed; the theme becomes rich and densely illustrated by the accumulation of different scenes and details. The reward for the gardener is exploring the theme in its many variations. A Japanese effect can be pulled off in a small garden corner, but there's pleasure in planting a hedge of bamboo as well as bamboo in a container, in designing a small dry Zen garden as well as a Japanese stepping-stone path. Sticking to one theme can be a way of having it all.

To create the biggest possible world, choose a theme that embraces the style of your house and the views from your garden into the neighborhood. The easiest theme to create will be the one that most suits your climate and the elements that already exist in your garden (see the section "Starting Points" near the beginning of each chapter).

Secondary Themes

Gardens that are obviously Mediterranean may also lean toward a formal, a natural, or a personal, eccentric theme, to accommodate your preference for order, your concern for the environment, or your sense of humor. Secondary themes like those enrich a theme garden with variation; they take it beyond a cookie-cutter or hallmark style; they make it your own.

Multiple Themes

Suppose you want tropical and Japanese and cottage—you can't narrow the choice down. Then consider how to create separate garden areas, one for each theme. You don't necessarily need lots of space for this. For example, you could set up the tropical garden on a roof deck or interior courtyard, the Japanese garden by a side door, and a cottage garden in the backyard. None of these areas need be large.

Other naturally discrete garden areas suitable for a change of theme are a gazebo or screened patio, the front doorstep or entrance

A Japanese theme, or any other theme, can be explored all through the garden and into the house *(above)* or adopted for just a doorstep or a side yard *(right)*. Note the bougainvillea on the wall; it's a linking plant. Pruned sculpturally it looks very Japanese, but over the wall it becomes part of a Mediterranean garden below. Design, right: Isabelle Greene and Associates.

garden, the space behind the garden shed, the short leg of an L-shaped area, a children's play spot, a sidewalk garden, the hardscape around a swimming pool, and the space beneath and between trees. You can also build a theme motel of garden rooms, creating the room walls with hedges, trellises, and fences.

If each garden theme has a completely enclosed space, you can do exactly as you please within that space; the banana leaves won't clash with the English daisies from any viewpoint. But when your areas are not entirely separate, think about how to link the themes.

Transitions between Themes

If you can see right into a tropical-to-the-nines patio from a cottage garden bench, then the spell of the cottage garden is broken. It's no longer a magical world of tumbling old-fashioned flowers; it's the ordinary everyday world of a mix of stuff. So the first rule of gardening with multiple themes is to protect your main viewpoints from spell breakers. Face the bench in a different direction, for example, or screen the edge of the patio. Have paths enter adjoining themes obliquely, so visitors can't see what's coming until they cross the threshold.

A threshold is a place of transition; it's here your guests will notice that the game has changed. You can make the threshold dramatic; for example, have your path leave a Mediterranean garden through a solid door in a tall wall to enter a tropical garden. It would be a complete surprise, assuming your guests hadn't spotted the palm tree peeping over the olive tree.

Thresholds may also be low-key. For example, you might choose a hedge (clipped holly would suit both areas) to separate a new formal garden from a Japanese garden, and put a wooden fence between a Japanese garden and a natural garden. Some thresholds are hardly recognizable as such, because the transition occurs gradually, with plants that suit both themes weaving together (see the photo at the right). Through the threshold area, you might change the paving gradually from, say, gravel to tropical-colored tiles set in gravel. For more ideas about linking, check the section "Links to Other Themes" in each chapter.

Theme Parks

Multiple themes can result in a garden that feels like a theme park. If you like that, well and good. If you want to avoid a theme park effect, here are some suggestions: Use very few if any striking sculptures, statues, and other garden ornaments; coming upon a gnome, then a Buddha, then a pink flamingo feels like a theme park. To create some sense of unity through many different themes, use a single paving material (say, concrete: pocked and colored for tropical, smooth and geometric for formal, broken pieces for natural). Keep your colors in a fairly narrow band, or repeat a color through the themes. Choose just one kind of tree (a fine-textured tree such as acacia or birch would work for most themes) so the views through the tree canopy pull the garden together.

This flower border might be the transition between a cottage garden and a tropical garden. The dahlias and daisies have a cottage style but are tropical in color, and some cannas, the icons of a tropical garden, are creeping into the mix. If you can make transitions like this, you don't need a hedge or fence between themes.

Patios, Decks, Roof Gardens

PATIOS, DECKS, AND ROOF GARDENS are generally close to the house if not attached to it. In thinking about suitable themes, you might consider such a space as an extension of the adjoining indoor room. For example, perhaps the room opening onto the deck has wallpaper or upholstery fabric with a leafy tropical pattern or a hot tropical color; building a complementary tropical garden outside the windows will enliven both areas.

A contemporary kitchen with lots of stainless steel might suggest a new formal theme for the adjoining patio, with steel mesh table and chairs. You might be able to use the same furniture indoors as outdoors, even the same floor material. Your rooms will look larger if they range out into the garden, and what a pleasure it is to be able to wander in and out of doors without changing your shoes.

A Mediterranean theme is popular for patios adjoining the house. In fact, a Mediterranean garden in the mind's eye comes complete with such a patio, sheltered by an arbor of grapevines or wisteria and surrounded by fragrant herbs and lavender. Mediterranean native plants generally grow well in containers, because they are adapted to hot, dry conditions. In contrast, if you choose a tropical theme, be aware that most tropical plants in pots need frequent watering, and the leaves of banana plants are easily shredded by wind.

A sanctuary theme works best in a quiet place, such as a roof deck or a patio off a bedroom. You need only sufficient room for a chair from which to watch the stars or the rising sun. A Japanese garden can be set up in very little space, too. Choose beautiful stones, and, if there's no room for lush amounts of greenery, install a small *tsukubai* (see page 38) or fountain for a sense of freshness.

Close to the house, arrange pots formally and choose colors to match the style indoors. At the edge of the deck, introduce a second theme by grouping pots more naturally and choosing plants that connect to a theme suggested by the view.

If your interest is in a personal, eccentric garden, consider mounting art and collections of objects on the exterior house walls. You might install shelves just as you would indoors. Instead of container plants, decorate the space with beautiful empty bowls or bowls filled with marbles or rubber ducks.

If a deck or patio or roof garden is your sole gardening space, there are ways to introduce a second theme. Partially screen a portion of the space with a trellis or a hedge in containers, and make a secret garden with a different theme on the other side. Take advantage of a niche in the house wall or a corner between walls; that might be a suitable place for a shrine on which to put flowers or a candle. Erect a canopy over part of the space and set up a different theme beneath it, partially closing the entrance to it with a pair of plants in containers or a bamboo blind. Select a birdbath and a plant that attracts hummingbirds or butterflies, and slip them into the sunny open side of the space.

A decorative screen or trellis can be used to create a quiet sanctuary at one end of a patio or deck. A pot of star jasmine (*Trachelospermum jasminoides*) creates a delightful fragrance in late spring and summer.

A retaining wall was built into a hillside to create this small outdoor dining area. The warm Mediterranean tones of the wall and floor and furnishings make the space cozy. Vines and a standard bay tree produce a luxuriant leafiness but take up very little floor space. Design: Linda Applewhite and Associates.

It's sensible to devote generous space on a city balcony to comfortable chairs and allow room for guests to get up, stretch, and take a tiny stroll to enjoy the view. The potted fig trees on this deck perimeter have a dual purpose: they bring fresh green life to an apartment high above the ground, and they provide some privacy from neighboring buildings. Design: Terence Conran.

Small Urban Gardens

A SMALL URBAN GARDEN may have some natural character that suggests a theme. If it has a warm slope, a Mediterranean garden might work well. If it's shady and has trees, consider a Japanese garden or a tropical one. If it has a view, look for suggestions there: perhaps borrow a neighbor's palm tree as a backdrop to a tropical garden, an Italian cypress for a Mediterranean garden.

Study your garden boundaries, because you save space if you don't need to screen them. Consider using a wall for a mural or a backdrop of plain bold color to enhance a particular theme. Think about a fence as a possible place for mounting a fountain or a collection of bonsai or found objects. You can open up garden boundaries by creating an illusion of the space continuing through them—set an interesting door and portal into a fence, or attach a mirror there. Maybe talk to your neighbors about sharing a window into each other's yards; consider the view as an extra theme, perhaps placing complementary plantings on your side of the window to foreground it.

The architectural style of your home will also suggest themes. Brick walls fit right in with a new formal theme, or a cottage theme if the house is modest in scale. Stone suits a Mediterranean garden. Wood works well with a Japanese theme; it also suggests a natural theme, but a natural garden, especially one with a sense of wild nature, is the hardest to pull off in an urban space—if you want to try it, choose the area at the end of the yard farthest from the house, and plant it so densely that the path looks overgrown, to heighten the sense of crossing out of the urban world.

The space at the end of the garden is an appropriate place for any second theme. Separate it from the main garden with a hedge, trellis, or tall shrub; choose an element that contributes well to your main theme. Because, in the mind's eye, the far end is wilder than areas close to the house, it's an excellent place for a sanctuary garden; it need only be large enough to accommodate a chair and a bubbling water fountain to override city noise.

Although urban yards are usually small, there's often a chance for another theme in a little space somewhere around the outside of the house. A flight of steps might be an opportunity for a Mediterranean garden, a front doorstep the place for a formal theme. If you have a deck, patio, or roof garden as well as a backyard, consider the ideas on pages 8–9.

At the end of a formal garden path, past flowerbeds and lawn, place an arch as a threshold to a second theme, such as a Mediterranean garden with a fountain and a simple place to eat alfresco. Create a butterfly and hummingbird garden, or a secret sanctuary garden, within the flowerbeds.

A tall blank wall is no longer where this garden in Globe, Arizona, ends. From flat concrete blocks, a tropical world has come to life, with a huge sense of space and playfulness. The tree foliage is for real—ice plants are trailing from pots situated on the top of the wall.

In a small yard, a natural theme can sometimes be pursued effectively beneath trees. Limit the choice of plants, to achieve a sense that they are colonizing naturally. Make paths small, like trails through undergrowth. Note the trimmed balls that link the natural garden here to a formal area. Design: Roger Warner.

Three pots, planted with coleus and purple fountain grass (*Pennisetum setaceum* 'Rubrum'), dress up a doorstep in Newport Beach, California. Repeating the plantings and coordinating the color of the pots with the flagstone paving create a formal effect. In the backyard, perhaps the coleus is found in a small tropical garden and the ornamental grass in a meadow.

Suburban Gardens

THE DREAM OF THE SUBURBS is outdoor space for everyone in the family—a play area for children, maybe even a pool and trees to climb, a place to barbecue and eat outdoors, a vegetable garden, perhaps an orchard, a flower garden, and a nicely kept entrance garden. There is room for many different themes in a traditional suburban garden; however, if you live in a modern suburban home where the house occupies most of the lot, you may have more in common with gardeners in small urban yards (see pages 10–11).

To give all household members their dreams, start surveying possibilities at the sidewalk and entrance garden. If local codes or neighborhood association rules don't mandate an open, unobstructed front yard, you could have both a formal theme and a sanctuary theme here, by setting a private courtyard behind a hedge or a screen of vines.

Side gardens are often shady places, but, if any morning sunlight comes near a bedroom opening into a side yard, make a sanctuary garden there. It will be attractive even if it's shady, as long as there's a view of sunlight from that spot. A side garden could be a Japanese garden, with small Japanese maples placed along a stepping-stone path. For interest, weave the path between the maples, set up a fountain or water bowl along the way, and site the trees so that there are pleasing views of them from the adjoining rooms of the house.

In the backyard, the standard choice, for convenience to the kitchen, is to set up a somewhat formal patio for eating outdoors close to the house. But you might like to be unconventional and have a dining area at the end of the yard; an outdoor meal will feel like more of an adventure out into nature there, and you could make the theme as natural or as fanciful as you please.

Beyond the patio is your acre, your chance to realize a personal dream. You might buy or build a small structure such as a gazebo, drape it with vines, and develop a theme inside that takes visitors completely by surprise. Out in the open, you might have sufficient space to create a natural habitat—a wildlife pond, for example, or a slice of woodland with native trees and understory shrubs.

Creating a large garden can be as daunting as furnishing a large house. Proceed room by room, theme by theme, paying particular attention to linking neighboring themes (see pages 6–7). The greatest challenge of a suburban garden is its large range of possibilities. It may quickly come to look like a theme park unless you determinedly take some simple measures to unify your garden, such as choosing just one paving material (see page 7).

To accommodate many themes, use the front garden and side yards as well as the backyard. If the backyard is large enough, separate it into three parts: for example, an area of lawn and paving for entertaining near the house; perhaps a pool and pool house or a natural garden at the far end of the yard; and, to one side, a vegetable garden with a small bed for flowers and a private seat.

This garden *(right)* is not large, but it contains many different rooms, some big enough to be shared by the family, others designed for a quiet conversation or a solitary retreat. Note how much effect is achieved at the threshold, in the design of the gate. Seven fountains unify the garden as a place of beautiful sounds. Design: Maria del Carmen Calvo.

A lath house with stained glass panels provides a quiet sanctuary that seems far from all the activity in the rest of the garden. Imagine beams of colored light flickering over your book and tea. Design: Jonathan Baillie.

Although a suburban garden has room for many themes, consider using a large part of the space to develop one theme luxuriantly. In the Beard garden, shown here, designers Glenn Withey and Charles Price chose plants that grow and bloom at different times, to keep the show going through the seasons.

Mediterranean Gardens

A Mediterranean garden is warm, dry, and fragrant with lavender, lemons, rosemary, and olives. Terra-cotta pots, tile mosaic, and seashells decorate the patio, paths, walls, and steps. A fountain cools the air. And there's a place to eat outside, with the table and chairs oftentimes set on gravel in the shade of a tree or under a rustic arbor of grapevines.

Give a patio a grand Mediterranean presence by planting a semicircle of Italian cypresses.

TALL, DARK, PENCIL-THIN

Italian cypresses are a popular Mediterranean landmark. Use a line of them to flank a bench or frame a view *(above)*. Or, to transform a plain suburban house into a Mediterranean-style home, paint the walls a soft pinkish beige clay color, and set two cypresses at the front entrance *(right)*. Design, right: gardenmakers.

If you have any of the following already in your garden, use it as a starting point for a Mediterranean garden:

- lavender
- Italian cypress
- olive or citrus tree
- herb or kitchen garden
- gravel or stone patio
- stone or stucco fountain
- large terra-cotta, stone, or stucco pot or trough
- rustic arbor
- terra-cotta-colored wall

A Mediterranean garden is an excellent choice for a sunny courtyard or a dry hillside.

MANY PLANTS NATIVE to the Mediterranean, such as pride of Madeira *(above)*, with its giant blue flower spikes, and snow-in-summer, creeping onto the path, have gray-green or silvery foliage (see pages 26–27). Place warm-colored boulders among them to evoke a sun-baked Mediterranean hillside. Design: Heide Stolpestad Baldwin.

BOUGAINVILLEA SPILLING OVER a white wall gives you a classic Mediterranean look. In hot, bright climates, however, be wary of painting too many surfaces white, or using white gravel, because of the glare. Design: Isabelle Greene and Associates.

A MEDITERRANEAN *potager* (kitchen garden) provides items for a simple alfresco lunch. To make best use of a small space, grow climbing crops (grapes, runner beans, or the like) on vertical surfaces, and set out terra-cotta pots filled with more plants on the path. In a cold-winter climate, you can bring pots of frost-sensitive plants indoors (see page 26).

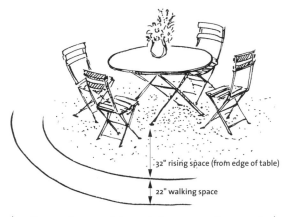

32" rising space (from edge of table)

22" walking space

Allow at least 4½ feet of clearance all around an outdoor table. With generous room, the space will feel more comfortable.

TERRA-COTTA-COLORED WALLS and roof tiles are hallmarks of Mediterranean style. So are outdoor dining areas adjoining the house. In summer, this small courtyard *(above)* is shaded with grapevines; a farmhouse patio *(right)* receives dappled light filtering through roses and wisteria. In winter, the plants lose their leaves, and the patios are warmed by the sun.

IN HOT-SUMMER climates, encourage visitors to walk through the garden by providing a shady destination such as this simple wooden arbor covered with three varieties of grapes in Janet Dindia's garden. Fragrant rosemary and honeysuckle surround the terrace.

IN MEDITERRANEAN GARDENS, the most common construction material is stone. To soften and decorate a stone courtyard, grow ferns and trailing plants in the walls, and arrange pots and troughs of many other plants on the floor (below). A hillside entrance garden (right) shows a different approach: boulders and roughly cut pieces of local stone with beautiful colors are the decorative elements. Design, right: Jack Chandler Associates.

YOU CAN MAKE A VIEW that's almost as cooling to the eye as the Mediterranean sea with these drought-tolerant misty blue plants *(below)*. The grass that looks like water vapor is *Muhlenbergia capillaris*; behind it is Mexican bush sage *(Salvia leucantha)*; in front of it is *Trachelium caeruleum*, a Mediterranean native, and, in the foreground, catmint *(Nepeta × faassenii)*. A dry Bacchus wall fountain surrounded by shells and coral in Sid Dickens's garden *(right)* also conjures thoughts of the sea. (To make a Mediterranean-style shell pot, see page 23.)

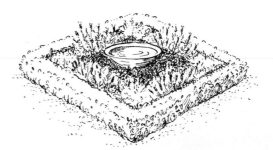

Use a simple, large water bowl to make a centerpiece for a Mediterranean herb garden.

IN AN ARID MEDITERRANEAN summer climate, the sound and sight of water are particularly refreshing. A single-basin fountain loses less water to the air than the multitiered fountains commonly available. Here, the spilling water runs prettily across the gravel courtyard in a stone channel, called a *rill*. Design: Jonathan Plant and Associates.

Here are some ways to settle your Mediterranean garden alongside a part of your garden with a different theme. For more information, see pages 4–13.

To link a Mediterranean garden to a Japanese garden, choose the same boulders and stone for both areas. To create continuity with a natural garden, plant a few ornamental grasses in both. Plant lavender to tie a Mediterranean garden to a cottage garden or sanctuary garden. If you have large terra-cotta pots in your Mediterranean garden, repeat them in a new formal garden. Mediterranean-style brightly colored tiles and seashells also work well in tropical and personal gardens.

IF YOU CHOOSE ORNATE POTS and plant them with a variety of showy plants, the effect tends to get giddy. Consider instead simple plantings for ornate containers, such as these little sedums and semper-vivums or a single *Phygelius* 'Tommy Knockers' *(above)*. Easiest of all are plain containers simply planted and placed for effect atop pedestals and walls *(right)*.

Mulching with Gravel

Mediterranean garden beds are often mulched with gravel for several reasons. A 2- to 3-inch layer of gravel reduces evaporation and holds moisture in the soil. At the same time it prevents moisture from accumulating around the crowns of plants, which can cause rot. Gravel helps prevent weed growth, saving on maintenance. Using both gravel mulch on planting beds and gravel surfaces on paths and terraces gives the garden a more uniform appearance. And gravel sets off plants beautifully.

Gravel may be rounded stones occurring naturally, such as pea gravel, or angular pieces manufactured by mechanically crushing large stones. Either sort works well for mulching and for paths, but crushed gravel packs together better than rounded stones, making firmer paths that are easier to walk on. A ⅜-inch gravel is useful for mulching and for paths. Select a pale color, such as light tan, that flatters plants and does not glare in bright sunlight. For information on purchasing gravel, see page 27.

Some gardeners install landscape fabric before planting (unlike plastic, this fabric is porous, allowing water and air to reach the soil). Gravel is then spread to cover the fabric. Landscape fabric blocks weed growth more effectively than gravel alone; however, as the gravel shifts about, the fabric may show through.

Harvesting and Drying Lavender

You can easily preserve the sweet scent of lavender by drying the flower stems. Then use them to make fragrant wreaths, or show them off in a vase. Dried flowers are traditional components of potpourri, sachets, and herb pillows.

Harvest the lavender when the lower third of the flowers have opened and their purple color is evident. It's best to cut the stems in the morning, before hot sun begins to wilt them. Either fasten the stems in bunches with rubber bands, and hang them upside down with twine in a dry area with good air circulation, or lay the stems on screens to dry. Drying them in a dark place, such as an attic, helps preserve the flower color.

Attaching Wall Pots

The Mediterranean region abounds with wonderful vertical gardens: centuries-old walls covered with foliage and flowers spilling from pots. Re-create this idea using either specially made flat-backed wall pots or regular round clay pots with rims.

Avoid walls exposed to drying winds, long periods of hot sun, or heavy shade. Choose a wall that is strong enough to support the weight of filled pots and that won't be damaged by water draining from them.

Flat-backed wall pots usually come with holes or brackets for screws or hooks; if necessary you can drill holes, using a masonry bit. Round pots can be suspended from metal rings, which also come with holes. Ask at a hardware store for the appropriate hardware to attach pots or rings to your wall surface—wood siding and masonry walls require different sorts of hardware from one another.

Making Mosaic and Shell Pots

Decorating plain terra-cotta pots with bright tiles or natural shells is a quick way to add an authentic Mediterranean touch to your patio or garden. A new pot is best for this project; it will accept the adhesive better than an old or stained pot. Use thinset mortar (latex-modified thinset is best for mosaics) and sanded grout (the grout recommended for mosaics with gaps of more than ⅛ inch between tiles); you'll find them at tile stores. Follow the label directions, and wear protective gloves when working with thinset or grout.

MOSAIC POT

Porcelain tiles intended for exterior use will last longer than interior tiles. You might also use bits of glass, stained glass, mirror, or marbles.

1. Fasten a strip of masking tape under the pot's lip to keep that area clean after you apply the tiles. Place the tiles between several sheets of newspaper, and tap them with a hammer to break them into pieces.

2. Use an old kitchen knife to apply thinset around the pot's lip and to the back of each piece of tile. Affix the tile pieces to the pot's lip. Let dry as the thinset label directs.

3. Press a small handful of grout onto the surface of the mosaic, and rub the grout firmly, with a circular motion, into the gaps between the tile pieces. Let the grout set for 10 to 15 minutes.

4. Barely moisten a cloth, and rub it over the mosaic to compact the grout further and remove any excess. Once a dry haze has formed on the tiles, polish the surface with a clean, dry cloth. Remove the masking tape. Let the grout cure, following the grout label instructions.

SHELL POT

Collect shells yourself, or buy them at hobby stores, or ask for them at seafood restaurants. If necessary, soak them overnight in soapy water, scrub them, and let them dry.

1. Use an old kitchen knife to spread thinset thickly over one side or section of the pot. For most shells, a layer ⅓ inch thick should suffice; a bit more may be needed for large or heavy shells.

2. Arrange the shells in the thinset, pressing them in firmly. Fill in spaces around larger shells with small or crushed shells, pebbles, or beads. Let the section dry completely before starting on the next section.

Create a realistic miniature Mediterranean landscape in a container. While a stone or concrete trough is the classic choice, any large, weatherproof, well-drained container will serve. Select fairly small plants that are in scale with the container; you might want to include some that will tumble over the edges. A few choices are houseleek *(Sempervivum),* rockcress *(Arabis caucasica),* sunrose *(Helianthemum nummularium),* thyme *(Thymus),* and bulbs, such as grape hyacinth *(Muscari)* and dwarf forms of narcissus.

1. Before filling the container, place it where you want it—most will be too heavy to move easily once planted. Cover the bottom with a piece of window screen to keep the planting mix from spilling out the drainage holes. Fill the container with planting mix to within 1 inch of the top; a mix of one part packaged potting mix and one part coarse sand or gravel chips will ensure good drainage. Mix in slow-release fertilizer—half the amount recommended on the label, because Mediterranean plants need little feeding. If you wish, add a few larger rocks, buried slightly.

2. Arrange the plants, still in their nursery containers, to check positions. Once you are satisfied, dig a hole for each plant, slip it out of its container, and plant it. Mulch the surface with a 1-inch layer of gravel. Water thoroughly to soak the planting mix. Troughs dry out quickly in hot weather; be sure to water whenever the soil is dry.

Taking Geranium Stem Cuttings

In cold climates, geraniums *(Pelargonium)* perish if left outdoors in winter. To save them for next summer's bloom, either bring the whole plant indoors or raise new plants from stem cuttings taken in fall. The new plants will be ready for life outdoors when warm weather returns.

1. Take cuttings from healthy plants, choosing shoots with at least three nodes (the point where the leaves attach). With a sharp knife, cut straight across the stem just below a node. Trim off flower buds, flowers, and all but the upper few leaves.

2. Fill a clean container (such as a round plastic pot or a flat) with moistened rooting medium; good choices include a mixture of one part perlite and one part peat moss, or perlite alone. Make holes with a pencil in the rooting medium, and insert the cuttings 1 inch deep; to help prevent rot, leave enough space between cuttings so that the leaves do not touch. Firm the medium around the cuttings, and water. Place the pot in a warm place that has light but not direct sunlight. Water when the surface of the medium dries.

3. When new leaves appear, gently pull on the cuttings; if you feel resistance, they have formed new roots and are ready to be transplanted to individual containers. For each cutting, half-fill a clean pot with potting mix. Dig up each cutting with a fork and place it in a pot. Firm additional mix around the roots, and water. Place the pots in a bright area out of direct sun for a few days, then move them to a sunny windowsill. After more leaves appear, begin feeding the plants monthly with houseplant fertilizer.

Clipping Plants into Mounds

In the wild, Mediterranean plants are pruned naturally by the wind or by goats and sheep who feed on them. Without such controls, many plants quickly grow too large, taking up more than their allotted space and, in some cases, becoming woody and unattractive. Clipping keeps plants compact and encourages fresh new growth. Gardeners routinely clip artemisia, bush germander *(Teucrium fruticans)*, lavender, oregano, rockrose *(Cistus)*, rosemary, many sages, santolina, and thyme.

Clip either in early spring or just after the plants flower, using hand shears or hedge clippers. Before you clip, look carefully at the plant and its neighbors to decide how much pruning is needed. Then clip over all the foliage, creating a fairly even surface but not cutting back as far as leafless wood, which will not sprout new leaves.

Plants and Materials

Many of the plants grown in Mediterranean gardens are tough, with small, beautifully textured, subtle grayish, or even hairy leaves that conserve moisture and prevent damage from the hot sun. Boldly colored flowers—and, in some cases, fruits—provide bright accents. The plants described here require well-drained soil and full sun. Except as noted, they need little water and little or no fertilizer. Some are tender in the coldest climates (hardiness is noted in parentheses); these can be grown in containers and sheltered in winter in a cool greenhouse or indoors in a sunny window. For large, hard-to-move pots, try wrapping the container in bubble wrap and covering the plant loosely with floating row cover, a lightweight fabric, sold in rolls, that provides several degrees of frost protection.

Plant grapevines for shade in summer and fruit in fall.

Artemisia

Providing a distinctive soft gray-green note to the Mediterranean garden, southernwood, *A. abrotanum* (−20°F/−29°C), is shrubby, to 3 feet tall and wide, with feathery, lemon-scented foliage. The smaller common wormwood, *A. absinthum* (−30°F/−22°C), grows 2 to 4 feet tall and 2 feet wide, featuring silver-gray, finely divided leaves with a bitter taste and pungent odor.

Bearded Iris

Tall bearded irises (−30°F/−34°C) contribute a wealth of elegant springtime flowers on 2½- to 4-foot stems over fans of swordlike leaves. Blooms are available in every color but pure red and green.

Citrus

Citrus trees (most 25°F/−4°C) are prized almost as much for their fragrant flowers and glossy evergreen foliage as for their delicious fruits. Some smaller-growing citruses do well in containers; good choices include 'Improved Meyer' lemon (grafted onto a dwarf rootstock), calamondin (produces hundreds of tiny, juicy, sour fruits that are good in marmalades), and kumquat (hardy to about 18°F/−8°C and bears small tangy fruits with sweet rinds). Water regularly and fertilize monthly.

Geranium *(Pelargonium)*

Bright and bountiful, geraniums (25°F/−4°C) spill from pots on patios, steps, railings, and walls. Bushy common geranium (*P. × hortorum*) grows 1 foot or more in height; some forms have zonal markings on the leaves. Ivy geranium (*P. peltatum*) produces trailing, branching stems. Both species bear glowing clusters of flowers in all the bright colors and white. Water and fertilize regularly. To overwinter geraniums as cuttings, see page 25.

Grape *(Vitis)*

Planted to cover an arbor, grapevines provide welcome shade plus clusters of tasty fruits; in winter their bare trunks offer architectural interest. The traditional Mediterranean species, *V. vinifera* (about 5°F/−15°C), produce many sorts of table and wine grapes. American grapes (such as slipskin 'Concord', which stems from *V. labrusca*) and various hybrids are more cold tolerant: −15°F/−26°C, some lower.

Italian Cypress
(Cupressus sempervirens 'Stricta')

A classic Mediterranean landscape tree, Italian cypress (0°F/−18°C) forms a a dense, narrow, evergreen column as high as 60 feet but only 5 to 10 feet wide at maturity. 'Glauca' has blue-green foliage.

Olive (Olea europaea)

An ancient symbol of peace and plenty, the olive tree (15°F/–9°C) is evergreen, with gray-green willowlike foliage. The smooth gray trunk and branches become gnarled and picturesque with age. The fruit ripens late in the year, but it is edible only when cured or pressed for oil, and it can be messy when it drops. Dwarf olives can be grown in containers.

Quaking Grass (Briza maxima)

This annual ornamental grass grows 1 to 2 feet tall with a delicate, graceful form. In summer it bears clusters of nodding, heart-shaped, small green spikes that somewhat resemble rattlesnake rattles; they dangle from thread-like stems and quake in the lightest breeze. Plants turn straw colored in late summer.

Rosemary (Rosmarinus)

Native to seaside cliffs in the Mediterranean region, rosemary is tough and versatile. Plant forms range from prostrate (most 20°F/–7°C) to 6 feet tall (some 0°F/–18°C or lower); all have narrow aromatic green leaves and small clusters of blue flowers in winter and spring. Rosemary is an excellent container plant.

Santolina

With whitish gray leaves on woody stems, lavender cotton, S. chamae cyparissus (–10°F/–23°C), forms a dense mound to 2 feet tall and 3 feet wide; bright yellow buttonlike flowers are a bonus. Less hardy S. rosmarinifolia (0°F/–18°C) is similar but has green leaves. Both can be sheared to make low hedges.

Sunflower (Helianthus annuus)

Though native to the New World, annual sunflowers are widely planted in southern France. The classic form grows 10 feet or taller with yellow flowers the size of dinner plates. Many smaller varieties have colors ranging from white to light yellow, orange, and burgundy.

Thyme (Thymus)

An excellent container or edging plant (–25°F/–32°C), as well as a classic herb for seasoning, common thyme (T. vulgaris) is a shrubby perennial growing to 1 foot tall and 2 feet wide, with tiny gray leaves and white or lilac flowers in early summer. Mat-forming varieties include woolly thyme (T. pseudolanuginosus), with soft gray leaves; and aromatic, caraway-scented thyme (T. herba-barona).

Lavender (Lavandula)

Among the most loved of Mediterranean shrubs, lavender is prized for fragrant flowers and aromatic gray or gray-green foliage. Sweetly fragrant English lavender, L. angustifolia (–20°F/–29°C), is actually native to southern Europe. Its leaves are gray-green or silvery, and its flowers pale to deep purple, appearing in early to midsummer. Many varieties are available, growing from 8 inches to 2 feet high and wide.

More tolerant of humid summers, lavandin, L. × intermedia (–10°F/–23°C), grows 2 to 3 feet tall and wide, with gray foliage and light blue to violet flowers in mid to late summer.

Spanish lavender, L. stoechas (0°F/–18°C), forms a stocky plant, 1½ to 3 feet tall and wide, with narrow gray-green leaves and unusual rounded spikes of dark maroon flowers from spring into summer, topped by bracts that resemble rabbit ears.

Selecting Terra-Cotta Pots

Unglazed pots made of terra-cotta (Italian for "baked earth") are an essential component of Mediterranean gardens. For durability, ask your dealer for high-fired terra-cotta; it is less likely to chip or break easily and can withstand some frost without cracking. (Low-fired pots are more porous, allowing water to penetrate the walls; when the water freezes, it expands, causing the pot to crack.) In cold climates, choose a pot with smooth sides that is larger at the top than the bottom; this allows frozen soil to push upward. In a pot that narrows at the top, frozen soil can push only outward, often breaking the pot.

Purchasing Gravel

To find local dealers, look in the Yellow Pages under headings such as Quarries; Landscaping Supplies; and Sand and Gravel. Visit several suppliers to compare prices and delivery charges. Take home samples, and study their color, both dry and wet. Gravel is sold by the cubic yard or by the ton; the dealer can help you calculate the amount you need.

Japanese Gardens

A Japanese garden evokes the natural world. Its essential components are water and stone, the yin (soft, feminine, gently flowing) and yang (solid, masculine, invigorating) elements of the wild landscape. The sense of serenity that makes Japanese gardens popular, especially in small urban plots, is achieved mainly by tailored green shrubs and trees. Flower and foliage colors are used sparingly, to signal the changing seasons.

THE EPHEMERAL SIGNS of the changing seasons are highly valued in traditional Japanese gardens. Choose plants not just for their flowers but for the lovely ways snow rests on the branches, raindrops pearl along the stems, or light shines through the leaves.

A JAPANESE GARDEN often includes beautifully crafted everyday objects. Use a wood crutch, burlap, and rope *(left)* to make an aesthetically pleasing support for an oak tree succumbing to the forces of age and gravity. Wrap a stone with rope *(below)* to designate that a path is closed. Design, left: Ron Herman. Design, below: Julie Moir Messervy.

If you have any of the following already in your garden, use it as a starting point for a Japanese garden:

- natural stream or pond
- natural boulders with moss or lichen
- stepping-stone path
- gravel or pebble area
- maple tree
- flowering plum or cherry tree
- bamboo
- magnolia or pine tree
- azaleas, rhododendrons, or camellias

A Japanese garden is an excellent choice for a small shady green site. In a place with no plants or water and little light, you can create a gravel and stone garden.

CAREFUL PRUNING is a hallmark of Japanese gardens. Prune a specimen Japanese maple, *Acer palmatum (left),* so that the trunk makes an S-shape and you can see into the tree. Clip shrubs such as azaleas and boxwood *(below)* into mounds, so they look almost as solid as boulders.

Mie-gakure is a way of creating mystery: you keep a view hidden and then reveal it obliquely.

USE A THRESHOLD such as a bridge *(below)* or a gateway *(right)* to emphasize a sense of moving into the natural world. A traditional Japanese tea garden has several such thresholds to help guests leave the everyday world behind. Design, below: Ron Herman. Design, right: Shiro Nakane, Julie Moir Messervy.

A natural site for a Japanese lantern is a promontory; place the lantern atop a flat rock.

SET STEPPING-STONES (see page 37) off-center from their neighbors and in zigzagging sections to make a beautiful path. Consider tatami mats of pebbles (large stone slabs would work just as well) to encourage walkers to stop for a moment and take in a view of something lovely from that spot.

GROUP BOULDERS in a composition that's pleasing from the main viewing points. Set the largest boulder at the back *(left)*; place one or two smaller boulders to the side and in front of it, to make it seem farther away and therefore bigger; place low boulders or stepping-stones in the foreground. Bring small boulders *(below)* into better relationship with one another by placing them on an island of gravel, moss, or fine-textured ground cover. Design, left: Isabelle Greene and Associates. Design, below: Carol Mercer, Lisa Verderosa.

To enclose a small Japanese garden and make a pleasing backdrop, put up a bamboo fence, screen, or blind.

CALM WATER is well matched *(above)* with low flat rocks to suggest a quiet pool. Use craggy upright rocks instead to mimic a gorge and tumbling stream. In either situation, place similar rocks nearby in the garden to tie the water feature into the landscape. Design: Oehme, van Sweden.

FALLING WATER makes the most musical sounds when it splashes and drips off several surfaces. The Japanese countryside has many mountain streams; in the city, you can conjure the coolness and freshness of water in a small *tsukubai* (see page 38).

Here are some ways to settle your Japanese garden alongside a part of your garden with a different theme. For more information, see pages 4–13.

To link a Japanese garden to a tropical garden, plant bamboo in both. To create continuity with any other garden theme in this book, consider a gravel path; the gravel might contain rustic stepping-stones for the Japanese garden and a sanctuary garden, elegant cut stone for a new formal garden, handmade tile for a personal garden, or seeding perennials for a natural, cottage, or Mediterranean garden.

IN A JAPANESE gravel and stone garden, called a *karesansui (above)*, water exists only in the imagination. The eye follows rippling waves, raked with a special rake (see page 39), into the shores and through the isthmuses between islands. A modernist take on a *karesansui (right)* uses crushed glass instead of gravel and reintroduces the water.

A SHED OR HOME OFFICE at the bottom of the garden *(left)* can be given a Japanese touch if you choose wood shingles for the roof, varnished wood and split bamboo for the trim, and a shoji screen for a window or door. At the corner of this hut stands a tightly bound bundle of bamboo branches. Design: Masao Fukuhara.

Tying a Decorative Knot

Decorative and functional, special knots are used to fasten bamboo poles in fences, gates, and arbors; they also work well in smaller structures, such as towers or tripods to support climbing plants. Use rot-resistant twisted cord or twine, dyed black to contrast with the bamboo. This is a simple knot; more complex knots are also used.

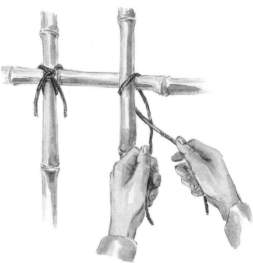

1. Cut an 18-inch piece of cord. Place it diagonally across the intersection of two bamboo poles. Pull the ends to the back, making them even in length.

2. Twist the ends tightly around each other behind the intersection. Pull the ends to the front at the other two corners of the intersection.

3. Tie the two ends securely with a square knot, and cut off the excess cord.

Containing Bamboo

You can literally watch some kinds of bamboo grow aboveground; unfortunately, they are simultaneously growing underground, sending out rhizomes (underground stems) in all directions. If not controlled, these running bamboos spread aggressively throughout your lawn and garden—and your neighbors', too. (Clumping bamboos are more restrained. This stand of mixed black and green bamboo is in Terry LeBlanc's garden.)

To keep running bamboo from running amok, confine it with 2- to 3-foot-deep barriers made from strips of galvanized sheet metal, 30-mil plastic, or poured concrete; specially made barriers are also available. Or plant your bamboo in long flue tiles, large plastic plant containers (with the bottoms cut out), or bottomless oil drums. Periodically check the surface for escaped stems, and cut them out immediately.

Making a Stepping-Stone Path

Tea gardens were developed in Japan in the early seventeenth century in conjunction with the tea ceremony itself. Stepping-stone paths guide guests through the garden to the teahouse, taking them on a journey away from the everyday world and helping them become calm and spiritually prepared for the ceremony to follow. It isn't necessary to install a complete tea garden to appreciate these ideas: a simple stepping-stone path leading to a secluded bench or a special view can also evoke a feeling of passage and a sense of calm.

For a stable path, select fairly large stepping-stones, at least 18 inches wide. They should be 3 to 4 inches thick, with a reasonably flat surface. Plan to place them only 4 to 6 inches apart; widely spaced stones make the walker hurry along, while close spacing slows the pace, subtly reinforcing the idea of taking a quiet journey.

1. To lay a stepping-stone path in soil, clear away weeds and level the area; If necessary, tamp the soil to make it firm. Lay out the stepping-stones on top of the soil, with the widest dimension of each stone horizontally across the path, rather than vertically. Try to cluster the stones in a natural way rather than placing them in an even, straight pattern.

2. Cut the soil around each stone with a spade or knife to mark its shape, and then move the stone to one side. With a spade, dig a hole 1 inch deeper than half the thickness of the stone; for example, if the stone is 4 inches thick, dig the hole 3 inches deep.

3. Spread 1 inch of sand in the hole, and wet it with a fine spray. Place the stone in the hole, and twist it into the sand, making it level and firm. If necessary, add more sand beneath the stone. Fill in around the edges with sand.

...ve feature of Japanese tea ...he *tsukubai* refers to a composition that includes a low-lying water basin attended by stones. Traditionally, as guests journeyed through the tea garden to the teahouse, they paused at the *tsukubai* and crouched to wash their hands and mouths, symbolically rinsing away the cares of the outside world.

To make a *tsukubai,* start with a basin; a hollowed-out stone is ideal. You may wish to set it on a wide, flat stone. About a foot in front of the basin, place the flat, low standing or front stone, about 16 inches in diameter. You kneel or squat on this to reach the basin. Just to the right of the basin, and within easy reach, place the setting-down stone, a flat-topped stone about 1 foot in diameter. This serves as a resting spot for a pitcher or teakettle with fresh water. To the left of the basin, position the slightly taller protection or candle stone. A candle or small lantern can be placed on it. Near these four main elements you can set smaller stones. Between the basin and the standing stone, spread water-worn pebbles to form a symbolic sea and help absorb spills. Finally, set a stepping-stone ahead of the standing stone, to lead to the *tsukubai.*

Fill the basin (from a hose) and the pitcher as needed. To integrate the arrangement into the garden, plant a few ferns and low grasses, with shrubs or bamboo in the background.

Candling Pines

Pruning shrubs and trees is an important aspect of the long-term maintenance of a Japanese garden. The goals of pruning include guiding growth in a desired direction, creating shapes and forms, and controlling size. On pine trees, new growth appears in spring in the form of spirelike buds; these are called *candles,* because that is what they look like until the needles open out. Candling—pinching back these buds—in spring as the needles start to emerge helps control and direct the growth of the branches. To promote bushiness and allow some increase in tree size, pinch out half of each candle. If you wish a branch to stop growing entirely, pinch out the whole candle. Pinch the candles with your finger and thumb, rather than clippers, which cut the tips of the emerging needles, causing them to turn brown.

Raking Gravel

A Japanese dry garden of raked gravel suggests water with its ripplelike patterns flowing around "islands" of stone. To hold the raked design of ridges and furrows, select gravel up to ½ inch across; you can also use turkey grit from an agricultural supplier. You need enough to make a layer about 4 inches deep. Though very light-colored gravel can be used to brighten a dark corner, pale gray or tan gravel is less glaring in a sunny site.

Before installing a gravel garden, clear weeds; you may want to lay down landscape fabric to prevent future weed growth. An edging of timber or stone helps contain the gravel. Spread the gravel evenly, wet it, and tamp it flat. To rake a pattern, walk backward, pulling the rake firmly through the gravel. Experiment with patterns other than ripples, such as straight lines, winding streams, checkerboards, zigzags,

and circles. After raking, water with a fine mist.

Unlike Western metal rakes, rakes for gravel gardens are made of wood and have longer, wider teeth, set farther apart. You can make such a rake by cutting teeth in a piece of ¾-inch-thick plywood; make them about 4 inches long, with either a V-shaped or a U-shaped pattern. Fasten a sturdy broom handle to the rake head.

Setting Large Stones

An arrangement of large stones is an important element in Japanese garden design. Stones can be selected to evoke a rugged mountain scene or a more gentle series of rolling hills. In either case, try to make the arrangement look as if it has been in place for a very long time.

For stability and a balanced appearance, sink most rocks into the ground by at least a third of their height. When setting a group of three rocks, start with the largest or central rock. Decide which side should face toward the main vantage point. Dig a hole and set the rock in place. Step back and check that it is where you want it. Then tamp soil firmly around the base of the rock. Place the next largest rock in the same way, making sure it is in balance with the first one; finish with the third and smallest rock. Smooth the soil around the rocks and add plants, if desired.

Plants and Materials

Plants in Japanese gardens are chosen to suggest scenes from nature. They evoke a timeless quality expressed through the emphasis on trees and shrubs; flowering annuals and perennials with their fleeting season of interest are of less importance. Except as noted, the plants described here grow best in average, well-drained soil and in full sun to partial shade; they need regular watering and feeding. Hardiness ratings are noted in parentheses.

Azalea (Rhododendron)

In Japanese gardens, evergreen azaleas are usually favored over deciduous ones; they are easily clipped into rounded mounds, while providing bursts of spring flowers. Kurume hybrids (5°F/−15°C) and the hardier Kaempferi hybrids (−15°F/−26°C) are both available in many colors. In colder regions, deciduous azaleas, such as Northern Lights hybrids (−45°F/−43°C) are a better bet.

Camellia

A large evergreen shrub, *C. japonica* (10°F/−12°C; some even lower) is the classic Japanese camellia, prized for glossy dark green foliage and beautiful flowers, which may appear from November through May, depending on the variety. *C. sasanqua* (5°F/−15°C) produces its scented flowers in fall. Some hybrids are hardier (−15°F/−26°C); among these, late-fall bloomers include white 'Snow Flurry' and pink 'Winter's Dream'.

Fern

Many ferns are well suited to Japanese gardens. Lady fern (*Athyrium filix-femina*) reaches 4 feet high, with thin, finely divided green fronds. Japanese painted fern (*A. nipponicum* 'Pictum') has 1½-foot-long fronds with lavender and silver markings (−25°F/−32°C).

Ginkgo (G. biloba)

Also known as maidenhair tree (−20°F/−29°C), this elegant deciduous tree has fan-shaped light green leaves that turn golden yellow in autumn. Ginkgoes can grow to 80 feet, but most mature trees top out at 35 to 50 feet; width is ½ to ⅔ of height. Plant male trees; females produce messy, ill-smelling fruit.

Heavenly Bamboo
(Nandina domestica)

Though not related, this plant is reminiscent of bamboo, with lightly branched, canelike stems and delicate foliage (0°F/−18°C). Most selections grow 6 to 8 feet tall and 3 to 4 feet wide. Leaves emerge pinkish and bronzy red in spring, become green in summer, and take on purple to reddish tints in fall.

Japanese Flowering Plum and Cherry (Prunus)

These related deciduous trees provide cherished displays of delicate spring blossoms. Japanese flowering plum, *P. mume* (−10°F/−23°C), is a long-lived tree growing to 20 feet tall and wide, with white, pink, or red flowers, depending on the variety. Japanese flowering cherry, *P. serrulata* (−20°F/

−29°C), is the species from which many varieties and hybrids of varying sizes have been developed. Flowers range from white through vivid pink.

Japanese Maple (Acer palmatum)

With a graceful branching pattern and wonderful fall color, deciduous Japanese maples (−10°F/−23°C) come in scores of varieties, offering choices in leaf shape, leaf color, and tree size. The species grows to 20 feet high, but some selections are much smaller and are excellent container plants.

Bamboo

Fast-growing members of the grass family, bamboo species are often planted as a backdrop to a *tsukubai*, as part of a raked gravel garden, or in containers. Popular running sorts, which spread widely by underground rhizomes, include 6- to 10-foot golden bamboo (*Phyllostachys aurea*) and 4- to 8-foot black bamboo (*P. nigra*). Kuma bamboo grass (*Sasa veitchii*) grows 2 to 3 feet high and is used as a ground cover. (All three are hardy to 0°F/−18°C.) For ways to contain running bamboo, see page 36.

Clumping bamboos spread much more slowly than running varieties. Among the clumping ones are the fountain bamboos, *Fargesia nitida* (0°F/−18°C), and *F. murielae* (−20°F/−29°C). Both grow 6 to 8 feet high and form airy, graceful plants. They grow best in shade.

Cutting Bamboo

To cut fresh bamboo, choose a regular Japanese pruning saw. A special finer-toothed bamboo saw is used to cut dry bamboo, producing smooth ends. Both saws cut on the pull stroke, allowing easy, fast cutting. On tying bamboo, see page 36. Bamboo saws and cord for tying are available from Gardener's Supply Company, www.gardeners.com.

The soft pink flowers of 'Hisakura' Japanese cherry celebrate the arrival of spring.

Mondo Grass *(Ophiopogon japonicus)*

A grasslike member of the lily family, mondo grass (0°F/−18°C) forms a dense clump 6 to 8 inches high, spreading slowly by underground stems. 'Kyoto Dwarf' and 'Nana' grow only half as large and are good choices for containers.

Moss

A carpet of moss makes a natural-looking ground cover in shady gardens, enhancing shrubs, trees, and rocks. Choose mosses adapted to your region. They are sold as plugs or sod and are easy to transplant. Some nurseries also sell dried and powdered moss; you sprinkle it over moist soil, tamp it in place, and water.

Pine *(Pinus)*

Important specimen trees in Japanese gardens, pines symbolize longevity and tenacity. Japanese black pine, *P. thunbergii* (−20°F/−29°C), forms a broad, conical tree, irregular and spreading with age. It grows to 100 feet high and 40 feet wide in cool climates, but is much smaller in hot areas. Shrubby mugho pine, *P. mugo mugo* (−40°F/−40°C), grows slowly, 4 to 8 feet high and 8 to 15 feet wide.

Star Magnolia *(Magnolia stellata)*

A slow-growing shrubby magnolia, eventually reaching 20 feet high, star magnolia (−20°F/−29°C) blooms profusely in early spring. Flowers are white or pink, depending on the variety. The blossoms may be nipped by frost in the coldest regions; 'Waterlily' blooms later than others, often escaping frost damage.

Yew Pine *(Podocarpus macrophyllus)*

An evergreen tree 15 to 50 feet tall and 6 to 15 feet wide, with bright green leaves, yew pine (0°F/−18°C) is a good choice for a screen or specimen plant. The much smaller shrubby yew pine, *P. m. maki,* 8 to 15 feet tall and 2 to 4 feet wide, grows well in containers.

Selecting Stones

Stepping-stones and large stones for special features are important elements in Japanese-style gardens. Take your time when selecting stones, checking various suppliers in your area. To find them, look in the Yellow Pages under Landscaping Supplies; Quarries; and Rock. On purchasing gravel, see page 27.

When selecting large stones for a rock grouping, look for sculptural pieces that complement each other in shape and color; think about their eventual arrangement in your garden.

Stepping-stones should be generous in size: look for stones at least 18 inches wide and 3 to 4 inches thick. Use just one type of stone for a natural appearance. Avoid stones with indentations in the center; if water collects there and freezes, the path will be dangerous.

Even a small amount of stone is heavy, so arrange for delivery. You may need to hire or rent heavy-duty equipment, such as a loader with a back hoe and bucket, to help move and place large stones.

Natural Gardens

A natural garden is alive with bees, birds, butterflies, and native plants that thrive in the natural landscape nearby. In moist regions of the country, a natural garden boasts tall green trees and vines; in arid regions, it might be a wash of desert flowers. Natural gardens are popular with children, because they are full of berries, husks, and seeds to collect and build with and long grasses or treetops, where children and small animals can hide.

Design, left: Oehme, van Sweden.

TO REPLICATE NATURAL plant communities, plant in layers, tall to low, tree canopy to shrubs to ground cover. If your garden is small, make sure that trees do not generate too much shade. On a roof deck, grow a tree in a large planter, and prune the branches to let plenty of light reach the deck floor. In a garden, plan a large open area next to trees (see page 42). Even in hot climates, people enjoy looking out from cool shady places to a sunlit scene. Design: Lee Galen.

To conserve rainwater for plant roots and prevent runoff, lay paving stones or bricks so that there are gaps between them.

A TREE HOUSE PROVIDES a special encounter with the natural world that's popular among adults as well as children. Make a house in between the branches of a strong, healthy, mature tree, or build one on stilts in the shadow of trees. Design: Lawson, Carter, Epstein.

If you have any of the following already in your garden, use it as a starting point for a natural garden:

- natural habitat, such as a stream, meadow, or desert wash
- native plants
- mature trees
- shrub or tree with berries
- wildflowers
- drift of bulbs
- ornamental grasses
- boulders
- logs or tree stumps

A natural garden is an excellent choice for a large yard or an unirrigated one; it's also a great choice for children.

YOU CAN BRING WATER, clouds, and treetops to a child *(above)* simply by setting up a container big enough for a toy ship in a place where the water surface will reflect the sky and a nearby tree or tall shrub; if you like, float parrot's feather *(Myriophyllum)* on the water. Keep a careful watch on very young children, because even as little water as this poses a drowning hazard. Design: Lawson, Carter, Epstein.

A LARGE YARD might be divided into a neatly cultivated area close to the house and farther out a more natural area that doesn't need so much maintenance, planted with wildflowers such as these poppies and bachelor's buttons *(below)*. In spring, fruit tree blossoms would draw people out here; in late summer and fall, they'd come to taste the harvest.

IN NATURE, PLANT COMMUNITIES are usually
quite simple, with one or two plants spreading into
beautiful sweeps. For a natural look in your garden,
choose just a few types of bulbs, such as narcissus
and Peruvian scilla *(above)*, and plant them in drifts
(see page 50). Or allow a couple of perennials or
annuals to spread by seed; purple globe thistle *(below)*
can also be increased by dividing mature plants.
Design, above: Benington Lordship.

MAKE THE MOST of a piece of naturally moist
habitat even if it dries in summer. Take a path to
it, and have people cross over ceremoniously on
a bridge, like this one over a stream obscured by
moisture-loving primulas. Consider adding a
tree, which will make the spot cooler, more
enclosed, and more enchanting. Note the log
edge to the plantings at the top of the photo.
Design: Bobbi Garthwaite.

IF YOU HAVE ROOM, set up a picnic table and benches in your natural garden, so you have a place to go out to, a special destination, for watching birds or the afternoon light fading to twilight. In a small garden, hide a chair or log among tall grasses and perennials as far away from house noises and chores as you can get; place a birdbath nearby (see page 52) to lure songbirds. Design: Oehme, van Sweden.

ORNAMENTAL GRASSES, such as this reed grass *(Calamagrostis)*, have become the classic plants of natural gardens. There are hundreds, including many native grasses. Some grasses are deciduous, some evergreen; some clump, some run; some have red, blue, yellow, brown, black, or variegated leaves; some produce lovely pink, golden, or buff flower plumes that persist into winter. Check out the height also, and be careful not to plant grasses that are so invasive they may spread to the wild. Design: Oehme, van Sweden.

If you have to cut down a mature tree, leave a stump about 18 inches high, so you can sit on it comfortably. Chip some branches to make a natural path, place log sections across the path to keep the chips in place, and consider turning any miscellaneous branches and pieces of plank into a chair.

A **NATURAL SEASIDE GARDEN** makes some use of materials at or close to the site—pebbles, fishing floats, and driftwood. Before purchasing new materials, take a fresh look at things around you to see how you might use them. You could make stepping-stone paths from pieces of broken-up concrete slab, for example; they would look quite natural in an urban or suburban setting.

SMOOTH RIVER-WASHED boulders serve as seats and lounging platforms around this secluded natural-looking spa. For any kind of rock project, choose local stone if it's available, because it will look more natural to the site than imported stone. Design: Hendrikus Schraven.

Here are some ways to settle your natural garden alongside a part of your garden with a different theme. For more information, see pages 4–13.

To link a natural garden to a Mediterranean garden, plant the same bulbs or grasses in both. For a Japanese garden, choose the same boulders and stone. A natural garden might meet a formal one where an uncut meadow turns to mown grass or a rustic stepping-stone path takes on a geometric pattern. To create continuity with a personal, eccentric garden, use native or local materials in both. Choose native plants with vibrant-colored flowers to tie a natural garden to a tropical one.

BUTTERFLIES CONGREGATE around this gate (*above*), lured by the yellow yarrow, yellow loosestrife, white and blue campanula, purple centaurea, and rose-pink foxglove. To attract birds to your garden, plant berried plants, such as cotoneaster (*below*), pyracantha, toyon, or viburnum. For more plant ideas for natural gardens, see pages 54–55; for information on feeding wildlife, see page 52.

To attract hummingbirds to your garden, choose plants with flowers that contain plenty of nectar, such as red penstemons and purple salvias.

A casual sweep of bulbs naturalized in a lawn or meadow, under deciduous trees, or in a lightly shaded woodland creates a lovely carpet of blooms. Best of all, with only a little attention from you, they bloom year after year, and the planting increases in size.

Bulbs need well-drained soil; in wet areas they may rot. Select plump, firm bulbs that feel heavy for their size; avoid any that are soft or moldy.

1. To naturalize bulbs, such as the daffodils shown above, traditionally you simply toss handfuls of them over the planting area, and then plant them where they fall. You may want to adjust the pattern slightly before planting. Make the drift denser toward the center, as if the bulbs began to grow in one spot and then gradually colonized nearby territory. Be sure the bulbs are at least their own width apart, to avoid overcrowding.

2. Whether you are planting in bare soil or in sod, use a trowel or bulb planter to make a hole for each bulb. For the preferred planting depths for favorite bulbs, see "Choosing Bulbs to Naturalize," on page 51. Mix a little bulb food or 10-10-10 fertilizer into the soil in the bottom of the hole; then drop in a bulb, and cover it with soil. Water enough to penetrate the soil

beneath the bulbs, where their roots will grow.

3. After the bulbs bloom, fertilize with bulb food or a 10-10-10 fertilizer. Even though you may need to delay mowing a meadow or cleaning up a planted area, it's important to allow the bulb foliage to remain until it withers; this helps bulbs build up nutrients for next year's show. Then mow or cut off the dead leaves.

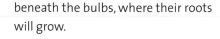

Choosing Bulbs to Naturalize

Plant spring bulbs in fall; plant fall-blooming ones in summer or early fall, when the bulbs become available. Preference for sun or shade and the best planting depth (depth of the hole) are noted.

Bluebell (*Hyacinthoides, Scilla*).

Spring. Light shade. Plant 3 inches deep in mild areas, up to 6 inches deep in very cold regions.

Crocus. Dutch crocus (*C. vernus*) blooms in spring. *C. speciosus* blooms in fall. Sun to light shade. Plant 2 to 3 inches deep.

Daffodil (*Narcissus*). Spring. Sun. Plant twice as deep as the bulbs are tall—5 to 6 inches for large bulbs, 3 to 5 inches for small ones.

Grape hyacinth (*Muscari armeniacum*). Spring. Sun to light shade. Plant 2 inches deep.

Meadow saffron (*Colchium*). Fall. Sun. Plant 3 inches deep.

Snowdrop (*Galanthus*). Spring. Light shade. Plant 3 to 4 inches deep.

Encouraging Natural Patinas and Mossy Surfaces

You can make a terra-cotta pot fit more naturally into the garden by accelerating the aging of its surface. Encouraging the growth of mosses makes both pots and rocks appear more natural.

PATINAS ON POTS

Newly purchased terra-cotta pots look rather raw and bright; with time, the surface gradually takes on a natural patina made of greenish algae or moss plus white deposits from minerals in the clay and potting soil. To make a pot look aged more quickly, you can set it in a shady, moist place, such as in long grass or under trees that drip rainwater. To make the surface greener, spray it several times with liquid fertilizer. Or soak aged manure, or leaves from the herb comfrey (*Symphytum officinale*), in water for a day or two, and brush the resulting

solution on the pot. Repeat the process several times.

MOSSY SURFACES ON ROCKS AND POTS

To encourage the growth of moss on rocks, terra-cotta containers, or cast stone pots, gather some moss from cracks in a sidewalk or a mossy bank. Crumble a cupful, and mix it in an old blender with a cup of yogurt or undiluted liquid fish fertilizer. Slather the solution onto your pot or rock, and set it in a shady, moist spot. If you must move a mossy rock or pot, wrap it in used carpet or foam padding to avoid damaging the moss.

Making a Natural Path

Whether paved with mossy stepping-stones, pebbles, or well-trod soil, paths—or trails—in natural gardens flow gently around or between other garden elements, rather than zigging and zagging aimlessly. You can install a curving bank or small berm on one or both sides of the path, as shown here, to create interest; this also hides the path from other parts of the garden and provides an attractive display area for plants. Clumps of ornamental grasses, trees, boulders, and groups of shrubs similarly provide logical reasons for turns and twists of a path. You can place objects such as a birdbath, a large pot, or a simple plank bench to signal turning places. For a dramatic effect, design a trail that curves out of view, creating a sense of mystery. Such a path draws people through the garden, to explore and discover elements hidden around each curve.

Providing Water for Wildlife

Offering sources of water is a sure way to attract birds and other creatures to your garden. A traditional birdbath placed on a pedestal or tree stump draws many sorts of birds and may bring squirrels as well. To provide some protection from cats and other predators, site the birdbath in an open area, 10 feet or so away from shrubs. The basin should be no deeper than 3 inches; sloping sides allow birds to wade in gradually, finding their preferred depth. A textured surface offers traction. Change the water frequently to keep it clean and inviting. In freezing weather, thaw ice with boiling water each morning, or install a heating element designed for birdbaths.

Hummingbirds may bathe in a very shallow birdbath, but they are more likely to take a shower by flying through the spray from a gentle waterfall, fountain, or sprinkler. A shallow water basin placed on the ground attracts some kinds of birds and is important to creatures such as toads, turtles, and rabbits, which don't climb. Butterflies congregate near a very shallow puddle or muddy area, taking in both water and minerals.

Providing supplemental food helps make your garden attractive to many species of birds. Set up birdseed stations in fall, and maintain them through winter when natural foods are scarce. Unless you plan to keep putting out birdseed through the warm season, gradually reduce the feed and then remove the feeders between March and May.

Locate feeders at varying levels to attract different species, and place them close enough to some kind of cover so birds can escape from predators—but not right next to shrubs where cats could lie in wait. Feeders need to be cleaned if they get wet or have seed stuck to the corners.

Mixed birdseed is available at the supermarket, but it often contains a high proportion of less appealing milo, rice, oat, or wheat seeds, which the birds may ignore. It's more economical and makes the birds happier if you buy the more favored sunflower, millet, safflower, and niger (nyger, thistle) seeds in bulk from a bird supply or feed store.

In winter, set out suet in special feeders or mesh bags; it provides essential fats to the birds.

A sugar-water mixture that approximates the nectar in flowers offers hummingbirds extra nourishment that is especially important when these active birds migrate in spring and fall. Hang feeders in shady spots that are safe from cats. To make the mixture, combine 1 part granulated sugar and 4 parts water in a saucepan. Boil for 2 minutes, then allow to cool completely before using. The nectar can be refrigerated for several weeks.

Clean feeders by rinsing them in warm water every few days; hummers can develop a deadly infection from dirty feeders.

Grown for their graceful form and wonderful textures, ornamental grasses require little care beyond routine grooming and occasional division. Grooming involves a cleanup in late winter.

REMOVING OLD GROWTH

Cut back dormant grasses (those that turn brown in winter), using pruning shears to trim dead foliage and flowering stems to within a few inches of the ground. If you have a number of large clumps, electric hedge shears or a mechanical weed trimmer will make quick work of this project. Clean up evergreen grasses every year by removing dead foliage, instead of cutting back; you can often "comb" out old growth by running your fingers through the clumps (wear gloves—some grasses have sharp edges). After a few years, however, these grasses may develop a great deal of dead foliage. Then, to encourage fresh growth, cut them back by ⅔ in fall or early spring.

DIVIDING CLUMPS

Divide ornamental grasses every few years, when the clump's center dies out or the plant becomes overgrown. Spring is the best time to divide grasses that become dormant in winter. Evergreen grasses can be divided in either fall or spring.

1. To make the clump easier to handle and reduce moisture loss, cut back the foliage by ⅓. With a sharp spade, dig all around the plant, loosening the rootball.

2. Pull or lever the clump out of the ground. Slice it into sections with the spade, a sharp knife, or, if very large and tough, an axe. Replant the outer sections, which will grow vigorously; discard the dead center of the clump.

Plants and Materials

Choosing plants for natural gardens often goes a step beyond simply looking for attractive form, foliage, and blossoms. Plants also provide food and shelter for birds, butterflies, butterfly larvae, bees, other beneficial insects, and various other creatures. To attract a wide range of wildlife, aim for a diverse selection of plants, including tall trees, thorny and fruit-bearing shrubs, grasses, and an array of flowering plants to provide nectar and pollen during as much of the year as possible. It's a good idea to emphasize native plants, since they're familiar to the local wildlife and adapted to your climate. Except as noted, the plants listed here grow in full sun to partial shade and require little water or fertilizer. Hardiness is noted in parentheses.

The abundant red fruits of 'Winter King' green hawthorn (Crataegus viridis) *provide a cool-season feast for avian visitors.*

Butterfly Weed *(Asclepias tuberosa)*

An important plant for butterflies, supplying both nectar for adults and food for larvae, perennial butterfly weed (−40°F/−40°C) sends up new stems from a dormant root each spring. The stems grow into a clump about 3 feet tall and 1 foot wide, topped with flattened clusters of vivid orange flowers in midsummer.

Columbine *(Aquilegia)*

Columbines (−40°F/−40°C) are perennials with lacy foliage and intricate, delicate flowers carried on slender, branching stems. Rocky Mountain columbine (*A. caerulea*) grows 1½ to 3 feet tall; its blue-and-white flowers with long spurs appear in spring and summer. Reaching about the same height, Western columbine (*A. formosa*) produces nodding red-and-yellow flowers with red spurs. Columbine flowers are attractive to

hummingbirds; the seeds are relished by many small birds.

Coreopsis

The bright, sunny daisy flowers of coreopsis invite butterflies to the garden; the seeds that follow nourish birds in fall and winter. Annual coreopsis (*C. tinctoria*) is a slender, upright 1½- to 3-foot-tall plant. From summer to fall, the flowers appear in yellow, orange, maroon, and bronze, banded with contrasting colors. The stems of perennial coreopsis, *C. lanceolata* (−40°F/−40°C), grow 1 to 2 feet high, with tufts of foliage at the base; the yellow flowers bloom in late spring and summer.

Crabapple *(Malus)*

Crabapples are deciduous trees or shrubs (−30°F/−34°C, most species) valued for their lavish springtime

show of white, pink, or red flowers followed by small fruits, much enjoyed by birds in fall and winter. Most grow about 25 feet high, though a few are smaller. Some older varieties are susceptible to diseases; look for resistant varieties.

Dogwood *(Cornus)*

Trees or shrubs, most dogwoods are deciduous. They provide beautiful spring flowers, fall foliage color, and late-season fruits for birds; colored stems on some also brighten the winter scene. Many harbor insects, offering further food for birds. In hot climates, dogwoods need partial shade. (Hardiness varies; check local sources for well-adapted varieties.)

Goldenrod *(Solidago rugosa)*

From late summer into fall, perennial goldenrod (−40°F/−40°C) brightens the garden with glowing flowers on arching, wide-branching stems. This plant can reach 5 feet in height, but a smaller cultivar, 'Fireworks', tops out at about 3 feet. Butterflies enjoy the flowers, and birds gobble up the seeds in late fall.

Hawthorn (Crataegus)

These small to medium-size deciduous trees (–20°F/–29°C, most species) offer a cloud of springtime flowers (typically white, single blossoms), colorful autumn foliage, and clusters of decorative fruits relished by many birds in fall and winter. Double-flowered selections generally don't produce fruit. Hawthorns are dense and thorny, providing shelter and nesting sites.

Juniper (Juniperus)

Like other needle-leafed conifers (such as pine, cypress, and spruce), junipers (–30°F/–34°C, most species) offer year-round shelter for birds and other creatures. Some birds also eat the berries. Junipers range from low-growing ground covers to shrubs to large trees. Foliage colors include shades of green, blue, gray, and yellow.

Oak (Quercus)

Oaks are a diverse group, from large shade trees to small ones. All bear acorns—an important food for birds and other wildlife. The oak foliage canopy provides good nesting sites and often harbors insects, another food attracting birds. Species include evergreen oaks for mild climates and deciduous ones for both cold-winter and milder regions (hardiness varies by species).

Purple Coneflower
(Echinacea purpurea)

A trouble-free, easy-to-grow perennial, purple coneflower (–40°F/–40°C) bears showy, 4-inch-wide daisies with dark, beehive-shaped centers and drooping, rosy-purple petals. Flowering stems rise 2 to 4 feet above clumps of bristly foliage. The flowers are a magnet for butterflies, the seeds that follow are favored by small birds.

Yarrow (Achillea)

From 1-foot-tall pastel varieties to bright yellow 5-footers, perennial yarrows (–40°F/–40°C) are carefree, generous bloomers. Most species have aromatic, finely dissected gray or green leaves. The flowers are tiny daisies packed into flattened heads; they make a good landing pad for butterflies (see the photo on page 43) and offer nectar throughout a long season in summer and autumn.

Wildflower Seeds

Seed mixtures said to grow in all regions often don't succeed. Look for ones geared to your region, or make your own from local wildflower seeds. Most grow best in sun, but mixes for partial shade are available. Check local nurseries and mail-order sources (www.wildseedfarms.com and www.plantsofthesouthwest.com are two possibilities). Before planting, cultivate and remove weeds, as you would for any garden bed. Plant as directed on the package; be sure to water and weed through the growing season. (This colorful array is in Robin Hopper's garden.)

Organic Mulches

Organic mulches are once-living matter; they improve the soil and add nutrients as they decompose. Choices include chopped leaves, compost, crushed nut shells, grass clippings, pine needles, shredded bark, straw, and wood chips. Buy large quantities from landscape suppliers or smaller amounts at garden centers. Apply grass clippings in thin layers, letting each layer dry before adding another. Apply other mulches 2 to 4 inches thick. Use on paths and around plants but not over the plant crowns.

Ornamental Grasses

Ranging from ground covers only a few inches high to tall fountains of foliage that sway dramatically in the breeze, ornamental grasses offer texture and color, as well as food and nesting materials for wildlife. Blue grama grass, *Bouteloua gracilis* (–40°F/–40°C), grows to 20 inches high, with narrow, semi-evergreen leaves and oddly shaped flowers that resemble hovering mosquitoes. Idaho fescue, *Festuca idahoensis* (–40°F/–40°C), forms a dense clump of evergreen blue-green foliage to 14 inches tall; plant closely for ground cover. Switch grass, *Panicum virgatum* (–30°F/–34°C), grows into an upright 4- to 7-foot-high clump of narrow, deep green or gray-green leaves topped by slender flower clusters; the foliage turns light brown in winter. Alkali sacaton, *Sporobolus airoides* (–20°F/–29°C), makes a 3-foot-high clump of grayish green leaves. Showy plumes of pale pink flowers bloom in summer or fall; the plant turns beige in winter.

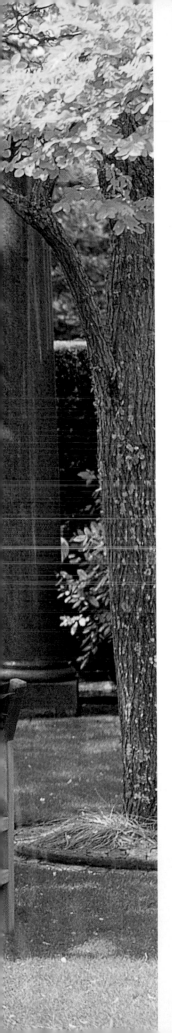

New Formal Gardens

A new formal garden is a modern take on the geometric and symmetrical gardens of France and Italy a hundred or more years ago. It celebrates strong lines, bold patterns, repetition of elements, and eye-catching forms, but it isn't rigid. The formality is purposefully disrupted by lively swinging lines, loose romantic plantings or wild nature, casual furniture, contemporary materials and objects, and bright modern colors.

Designs, above: top left, Claire Whitehouse; bottom right, Mia Lehrer.

COLOR, INSPIRED BY Indian saris, pops this classically simple arrangement of trees, walls, and gravel into the twenty-first century. To introduce bold color, either start with a swatch of paint and shop for plants whose foliage and flowers go gorgeously with it; or take your paint charts out to a wall or fence, and find a color to put behind a favorite plant. In a small urban garden, consider using bright color to draw attention away from an unattractive view. Design: Topher Delaney.

THIS LITTLE TERRACE in a steep garden provides enough room for a grand effect. The clipped boxwood knot, ivy walls, and sculpture are quintessentially formal, but untamed plants have been allowed to range over the lines to lend a lively sense of mischief. You could also make a knot garden less formal by letting the plants inside jump over the outline into the gravel.

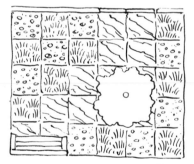

A strong ground pattern delights the eye. It is especially effective when seen from a deck or window overlooking the garden. At top, squares of slate, set into a checkerboard floor of grass and pebbles, lead to a bench. At bottom, a gravel path loops around an island bed.

HERE'S EVIDENCE *(above)* of how much fun formal geometry can be if you are bold enough to break down some of its boundaries. Old-fashioned parterres were clearly not meant to be entered; this wire-framed box-wood woman ignores that taboo. The purple and the green-variegated parterre plants are varieties of sage (for ideas on other bedding plants, see page 67).

If you have any of the following already in your garden, use it as a starting point for a new formal garden:

- clipped hedge
- plants set out in rows or a grid
- flat growing area, for a parterre
- rectangular, circular, oval, or elliptical pond
- formal lawn
- formal paving
- pillars or columns
- garden wall
- pattern, such as checkerboard tiles or pavers

A new formal garden is an excellent choice for an entrance garden and any area next to strong architectural lines.

YOU CAN MESS WITH a traditional parterre (see page 67) in umpteen ways to make it modern. Reimagine it with dwarf ornamental grasses and contemporary materials such as glass pebbles *(above)*. Or plant some of the pattern in turf *(right)* so you can walk through it and picnic on it—even, if it's a full checkerboard, play chess on it. Perhaps choose plants for each square that will grow to a different height; some might have prickly parts or mysterious smells. A chair could be set on one square. Because a parterre pattern is so strong, it continues to hang together through a fair amount of playful deconstruction.

LAWN IS A CLASSIC element in formal gardens. To conserve water, consider setting circles or squares of lawn in a floor of gravel or pebbles *(above)* rather than installing a full lawn; or run strips of lawn or another lush ground cover, such as baby's tears, across a striking pattern in a hardscape *(right)*. Design, above: Mia Lehrer. Design, right: Mathew Henning.

THESE STEEL TOWERS and stucco wall have as much presence as geometric forms carved of boxwood or yew, but they are decidedly more modern, and they don't require clipping. Design: Steve Martino.

HERE, WAVY LINES reply to a beat of straight lines; some Mexican fan and queen palms form groups, others break away. The garden is all about rhythm; one of the owners is a jazz guitarist. Design: Mia Lehrer.

A DIZZYING KALEIDOSCOPE of reflected sky, treetops, and leaves glitters off the mirror tiles in and at the back of this small water feature, making it seem infinitely bigger than it is. The pictures are constantly changing in response to the wind and the sunlight moving across the garden. Design: Simon Harman and John Greenwood.

Formal lines serve as visual cues for visitors searching for a front door that's out of view.

WHERE A FORMAL AREA meets a naturally planted one, you have two choices: let the two confront each other *(above)*, which produces a sense of drama; or create a transition zone *(right, above and below)* where the order breaks down gradually. Design, above: Susan Van Atta. Design, right, below: Jack Chandler Associates.

A formal path, steps, and the low walls of raised beds can help settle a house into the site by continuing the lines of the architecture out across the land. For an elegant effect, use the same materials for the garden hardscape that were used for the house.

Here are some ways to settle your new formal garden alongside a part of your garden with a different theme. For more information, see pages 4–13.

To link a new formal garden to a Mediterranean garden, plant clipped shrubs in both. To create continuity with a Japanese garden or a tropical garden, use the same paving in both. A new formal garden can meet a natural garden in two ways; see the photos on page 62. To link a new formal garden to a cottage garden, carry a low boxwood hedge from one to the other. A formal wall or hedge might be continued from a new formal garden into a sanctuary garden to provide enclosure and privacy.

FAMOUS FOR THEIR BOLD, romantic designs, landscape architects Wolfgang Oehme and James van Sweden often marry a formal patio to wild-looking water and blocks of ornamental grasses.

A METAL WATER TROUGH and a stucco-and-rebar pergola bring some pleasing firm lines to a garden full of waving ornamental grasses; shadows of the grasses and trees flicker beautifully across them. Design: Janet Rademacker.

Painting a Wooden Planter

Wooden planters, often arranged symmetrically on either side of a garden entrance or along a path, are frequent elements in formal gardens. The elegant Versailles tub is the most popular style and looks especially appropriate planted with a boxwood topiary or a standard rose. The tubs are usually painted white, but to make an interesting variation you can paint them to match your front door or another architectural feature or give them a modern glossy black coat. (This one is in a garden designed by Lisette Pleasance.) If your tub lacks the classic round finials at the corners, add them before painting.

Sand a new, unpainted planter lightly, and apply a coat of primer; after it has dried, brush on exterior latex paint. If your planter is already painted, sand the surface to roughen it, and then apply the latex. In either case, you may need two coats of paint.

Growing a Boxwood Hedge

Formal hedges of boxwood lend an architectural, structured air to the garden, whether they define the edge of a bed, terrace, pond, or parterre. Depending on the variety of boxwood selected (see page 69) and the frequency of clipping, hedges grow from 6 inches to more than 5 feet in height.

1. Select a site in full sun to partial shade for your boxwood hedge. Plan to plant in spring; in mild climates, you can also plant in fall. Remove weeds in the planting area, and dig in compost and an all-purpose fertilizer. Mark the hedge line with string run between stakes. Set plants closely, generally 1 to 2 feet apart depending on the variety; check with your supplier. Water well, and spread mulch around the plants. To force new growth, which will make a dense hedge, prune immediately, cutting the branches back by about a third.

2. In spring of the following year, again cut back the boxwood by about a third; trim the side growth several times during the summer. The ultimate shape of the hedge may be rounded, boxy, or pointed at the top. However, any hedge more than a foot or so high should have sides that slope wider at the bottom. This allows sunlight to reach the entire hedge surface. If the lower branches are shaded, they grow more slowly and eventually die.

3. Once the hedge has reached the height you want, prune each year after the spring growth flush has stopped, to prevent the hedge from growing any bigger. A simple wooden frame made of 1-by-2 boards nailed together serves as a guide for shearing a hedge.

Growing Topiary

Creating boxwood topiary is similar to making a hedge. In both cases, early pruning forces dense new growth; once mature size is reached, clipping maintains the intended shape. Topiary shapes include formal spheres, columns, pyramids, and spirals, as well as whimsical animal or bird forms.

Training container-grown topiary is not difficult, but it may take a few years to complete. Either buy a frame, such as the wire cone shown

here, to guide the shape, or make your own with stakes and wire. Start with a naturally bushy boxwood plant in a gallon or larger pot. Transplant it into the chosen container. Clip it back by ⅓, making a general cone shape. The next year (or whenever the plant is large enough), place the wire frame over it, and clip the plant to shape.

Maintain the shape with frequent light clipping. The plant eventually grows to cover and hide the frame.

Making a Bed with Squared Corners

In formal gardens, the trees, hedges, and other plants are often set out in straight lines forming the sides of square or rectangular beds. Here's how to set up the boundaries for a bed with perfectly square corners. If you wish to set plants in straight lines within the bed, it is easy to make a grid by laying out parallel lines.

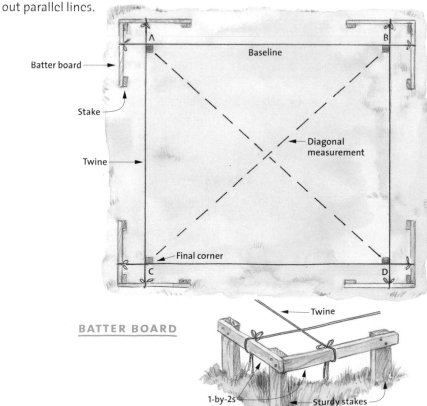

Baseline

Batter board

Stake

Twine

Diagonal measurement

Final corner

BATTER BOARD

Twine

1-by-2s

Sturdy stakes

1. Make four right-angle batter boards, using sturdy stakes for the uprights and 1-by-2 boards for the horizontal crosspieces. Set a batter board about 18 inches outside each corner of the bed, using a carpenter's square to estimate the corners.

2. Run twine between two adjacent batter boards to lay out a baseline, AB, for one end of the bed; loop the twine around the crosspieces, so that you can slide it to the left or right. Run twine to lay out the sides of the bed, AC and BD, and then another length of twine, CD, to complete the outline.

3. To make the bed square, measure the diagonal distance between opposite corners; adjust the lines tied to the batter boards until the diagonal distances are equal. Drive stakes where the adjusted lines meet, to mark the final corners of the bed.

Laying Out Circular and Oval Beds

In addition to precise square or rectangular beds, beds in circles and ovals—often situated in a lawn—contribute symmetry and order to formal gardens.

1. To create a circular bed, place a pivot post (a stake) at the center of the bed site, and tie a length of twine to it. Tie the other end of the twine to a pointed stick at the desired radius of the bed. Pull the twine taut, and trace the outline of the bed with the stick as you walk around the pivot post.

Pointed stick →

Pivot post →

Twine

2. To outline an oval bed, mark lines for two circular beds as described in step 1, and then join them with straight lines.

3. To carry this idea one step further, make a bed in the shape of two crossed ovals.

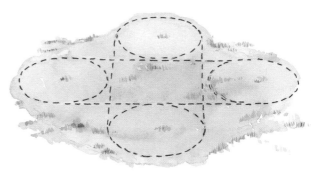

Creating Bedding Patterns

Large beds filled with ordered groups of colorful plants forming distinctive patterns were traditional components of formal Victorian front gardens. These beds often featured a central, taller dot plant or a decorative urn, surrounded by blocks of filler plants and edged with low-growing plants of a single color. These ideas are easily adapted to smaller modern gardens, where simpler patterns using just a few kinds of plants create a bold design.

Start planning a bedding pattern by working it out to scale on graph paper. For the most effective display,

CLASSIC ROUND BED

use fairly large blocks of the same plant variety. (See page 67 for lists of suggested plants.) Seeds sown directly in the bed generally take too long to grow to flowering size. Instead, most gardeners set out

plants from a nursery or start their own indoors in early spring. After digging in compost and fertilizer, pour sand from a bottle to mark your pattern on the soil. Set out the plants, starting at the center. After planting, be sure to water as needed and trim the plants regularly to keep them neat.

NEW WAVE BEDDING SCHEME

Creating a Parterre

A French word meaning "on the ground," *parterre* refers to a level space that contains formal ornamental beds, usually outlined with low, clipped hedges but sometimes edged with brick. Parterres may be filled with flowering plants, colored gravel, or glass pebbles. Designs range from fairly simple geometric triangles and semicircles to flowing, fanciful, scroll-like patterns and symbolic themes. Knot gardens are an English variant, designed with a continuous pattern of interlacing bands.

In knot gardens, the hedges often combine plants, such as germander *(Teucrium chamaedrys)* and lavender cotton *(Santolina chamaecyparissus)*. Gardeners delight in creating patterns for parterres and knot gardens; the three designs shown here will get you started (the brick-edged parterre is adapted from a design by Mary Zahl).

SWIRLING MODERN PARTERRE

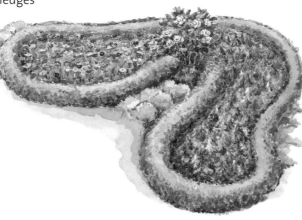

KNOT GARDEN

BRICK-EDGED PARTERRE

Choosing Plants for Bedding

Bedding plants are usually fast-growing annuals or short-lived perennials; select varieties with uniform, compact growth. Filler plants make up the main part of the design; some are grown for foliage rather than flowers. Low edging plants define the outer line; taller dot plants make a focal point, usually in the center.

FILLER PLANTS
Begonia *(Semperflorens* type)
Dusty miller *(Senecio cineraria)*
Floss flower *(Ageratum houstonianum)*
Geranium *(Pelargonium)*
Marigold *(Tagetes)*
Ornamental cabbage and kale
   (Brassica)
Petunia
Sage *(Salvia farinacea, S. splendens)*
Succulents (such as *Echeveria, Sedum, Sempervivum)*
Verbena *(Verbena × hybrida)*
Zinnia

EDGING PLANTS
English daisy *(Bellis perennis)*
Lobelia *(Lobelia erinus)*
Sweet alyssum *(Lobularia maritima)*

DOT PLANTS
Canna
Castor bean *(Ricinus communis)*
Giant dracaena *(Cordyline australis)*

Plants and Materials

Plants for new formal gardens are generally selected more for their contribution to the structure and framework of the garden than for their colorful flowers. Many plants can be sculpted into hedges or topiary through frequent clipping, while others naturally assume a symmetrical, orderly form. When flowering plants are included, they are often contained and restrained by lawn, hedges, or hardscape, such as paths or terraces, or they are assembled in a patterned bed. Except as noted, the plants described here require full sun to partial shade and average, well-drained soil; they need regular watering and feeding. Hardiness is noted in parentheses.

Bay *(Laurus nobilis)*

Also known as sweet bay or Grecian laurel, this shrub or small tree (10°F/−12°C) grows 12 to 40 feet tall and wide. Its aromatic, 2- to 4-inch dark green leaves are the traditional bay leaves of cookery. A classic formal container plant, bay can be clipped into topiary shapes. Where bay is not hardy enough, grow it in a movable pot, and bring it indoors in winter.

Beech *(Fagus sylvatica)*

Typically growing into a broad cone shape with sweeping lower branches, beech trees (−20°F/−29°C) can reach 90 feet tall and 60 feet wide, but are usually much smaller. The leaves are glossy, dark green, turning red-brown in fall; many hang on well into winter. Copper beech ('Atropunicea', often sold as 'Riversii' or 'Purpurea') has deep reddish or purple leaves. Beeches can be planted close together and trimmed to make a dense hedge as low as 4 feet.

Boxwood, trained to form dramatic topiary balls and spirals, as well as low hedges, makes a formal statement in this garden. Design: Jonathan Baillie.

English Ivy *(Hedera helix)*

English ivy quickly cloaks a wall or wire fence with dense, handsome, dark green, lobed leaves, making a serene background for other garden features. It also is a fast-growing ground cover that looks good all year. However, ivy can become invasive if not checked. Selections are available with variegated leaves and with smaller leaves; the latter are especially useful for covering wire topiary frames. (Most cultivars are hardy to −10°F/−23°C; 'Baltica' tolerates −15°F/−26°C.)

Holly *(Ilex)*

Most hollies are evergreen with spiny leaves. They grow into dense symmetrical shrubs or small trees and can be clipped to form hedges. Holly plants are either male or female; the colorful berries come only on female plants, but you usually need to plant a male of the same species to get berries. English holly, *I. aquifolium* (0°F/−18°C), grows slowly to 40 feet tall and 25 feet wide. Some selections have variegated foliage. The hardy hybrid *I. × meserveae* (−20°F/−29°C) forms a dense, bushy plant to 10 feet tall; some varieties have yellow berries.

Iceberg Rose *(Rosa)*

Many sorts of roses are cultivated in formal gardens, often planted in groups of a single variety, set off by symmetrical, dark green hedges. The floribunda rose 'Iceberg' is an especially good choice. Its fragrant white flowers bloom almost continuously on disease-resistant plants growing to about 6 feet tall. 'Iceberg' can be part of a traditional rose garden or, with plants 3 feet apart, can make a charming hedge. (Give floribunda roses winter protection where temperatures drop to 10°F/−12°C or lower.)

London Plane Tree
(Platanus × acerifolia)

A deciduous tree that reaches 80 feet tall and 40 feet wide, London plane (−20°F/−29°C) is too large for most gardens, but if it is pollarded (the entire crown is cut back severely each winter), it forms a low, dense canopy, suitable for smaller spaces. London plane is also amenable to pleaching (interweaving branches or training them on wires to form a dense wall or canopy of foliage). The lobed leaves of London plane are large and rough; the gray bark is handsome in winter.

Pittosporum

Pittosporums are easy-to-grow evergreens with dense, good-looking foliage and fragrant flowers. *P. eugenoides* (20°F/−7°C) is usually grown as a high hedge; unpruned, it can form a tree 40 feet high and 20 feet wide. The 2- to 4-inch-long leaves are glossy with wavy edges. Tobira, *P. tobira* (−5°F/−20°C) naturally forms a 6- to 15-foot-tall rounded shrub; it can be pruned to make a handsome hedge. The whorls of leathery leaves are glossy and dark green. Selections with variegated foliage and more compact growth are available.

Tulip (*Tulipa*)

Tulips bring springtime color to beds, parterres, and containers that later bear plants for summer and fall blooms. Tulips look most formal when only one variety is planted, so that they bloom at the same time and the same height. Red tulips are often favored for their contrast to low green hedges, although pastels work well, too. Tulips grow best in areas that have a distinct winter chill

Virginia Creeper
(*Parthenocissus quinquefolia*)

This vigorous deciduous vine (−30°F/−34°C) decorates walls and arbors with handsome foliage that is bronze-tinted in spring, matures to semiglossy dark green, and turns crimson and burgundy in early fall. Each leaf has five 6-inch leaflets with pointed tips. The stems attach themselves to supports with suction discs at the ends of tendrils.

Water Lily (*Nymphaea*)

The rounded, floating leaves and showy blossoms of water lilies give a classic elegance to formal pools. There are hardy and tropical kinds; both are usually planted in tubs placed on the floor of the pool. Easier to grow, hardy water lilies (−30°F/−34°C) go dormant in fall and reappear in spring. Tropical varieties go dormant in mild climates but die in freezing temperatures. In cold climates, store their tubers indoors in damp sand during winter.

Yew (*Taxus baccata*)

Slow-growing but long-lived conifers with dark green needles, yews (−10°F/−23°C) are important in formal gardens. They are favored for hedges and topiary because they take shearing and clipping well. If unclipped, English yew can grow to 40 feet high. Selections include 'Adpressa', a dense shrub to 5 feet high and 8 feet wide, and Irish yew ('Stricta'), which forms a column 15 to 30 feet high and 3 to 10 feet wide.

Selecting Cut Stone

Stone cut into flat slabs with straight edges suits formal gardens and makes a stable, safe surface for entrances, main walkways, and terraces. When selecting cut stone, check that its color complements the color of your house, garden furniture, and plantings. A neutral color, such as gray or brown, blends in easily and is well suited to a formal garden. Choose stone that is quite flat and regular in appearance; this is especially important if you plan to place outdoor dining furniture on a stone floor, as in this garden (designed by Conni Cross).

Some porous kinds of cut stone, such as sandstone, stain easily if sticky tree litter or berries fall on them. You can buy sealants to help prevent staining, but you must reapply them frequently. More durable, harder stones may be a better choice.

To find suppliers of cut stone, look in the Yellow Pages under Landscaping Supplies; Quarries; and Rock. Cut stone is sold by the square foot or by the ton. The supplier can advise you on how much to order. Buy extra stone to allow for breakage; it may be difficult to match the stone later.

Boxwood (*Buxus*)

A classic plant for formal hedges and topiary, boxwood features small, usually evergreen leaves that grow densely along the stems. Japanese boxwood, *B. micropylla japonica* (−10°F/−23°C), has ½- to 1-inch round-tipped leaves that are bright green in summer, but turn brown or bronze in winter in many areas. If unclipped, it grows slowly to 6 feet high. Korean boxwood, *B. m. koreana* (−20°F/−29°C), is noted for its ability to survive where others freeze. Its ¼- to ½-inch leaves are green in summer, yellowish brown in winter; plants slowly reach 2½ feet high. Common or English boxwood, *B. sempervirens* (−10°F/−23°C), has medium-size leaves that remain evergreen in winter. Plants can reach 20 feet tall if unpruned. Dense, compact 'Suffruticosa', or true dwarf boxwood, grows slowly to 5 feet in height but is usually clipped much lower.

Personal, Eccentric Gardens

A personal, eccentric garden is an exploration of whim.

Often it begins with using what you have at hand to edge

a path or make a pedestal for a pot, and then you find a

place for something too pretty to discard, and from there

you discover the pleasure of doing just as you please.

Common in personal, eccentric gardens are collections of

colored glass, shells, or found metal; some gardens become

inhabited—by a mosaic turtle or a year-round snowman.

Design, left: Bob Clark. Designs above: shell sculpture, Belinda Eade;
snowman, Roger Raiche; chair, Bob Clark.

IF YOU ARE self-conscious as an artist, start out by arranging your materials so that they have a function. Skis *(above)* are, after all, the approximate shape of pickets, so why shouldn't they make a fence. Old washers *(right)* look like gravel from a distance, so why not use them as a path surface (as long as they won't get super-hot and burn your feet).

THE LATE GARDEN DESIGNER and artist Harland Hand was particularly fond of concrete. He sculpted it into steps and stepping-stones and benches that, in their color and rounded edges, resembled natural rock formations. Between the concrete stones, he placed small plants—soft pretty gray ones, like lamb's ears *(Stachys)* and hen and chicks *(Echeveria)*, to take the chill off the concrete, and contrasting dark green ones, such as mondo grass, to accentuate the lines of the stones. For more information on his method, see page 79.

Instead of placing individual rocks or bowling balls around the garden, collect them into a pyramid to make a more dramatic display. For other ideas on arranging stones (and plants), see pages 78 and 81.

PAVING IS A wide-open canvas for an eccentric gardener. Marcia Donahue etched these skulls into old bricks with an electric grinder. Elsewhere in her garden, she has sunk horseshoes into wet concrete and written in it with a file or screwdriver. On personalizing concrete, see page 79.

If you have any of the following, use it as a starting point for a personal, eccentric garden:

- bottle, glass, or shell collection
- sentimentally valued objects, such as children's art or toys
- metal junk
- architectural salvage, such as window frames, columns, pieces of facade
- lots of one particular item, such as old skis, bowling balls, or shoes
- tools or machinery for tumbling glass or engraving concrete

A personal, eccentric garden is an excellent choice for a small garden or a drab area of a yard. It's perfect for creative gardeners, including children, and gardeners on a low budget.

TO STIMULATE children's creativity and interest them in gardening, suggest that they help you prune a tree, and then give them the cut branches to use in designing a playhouse. Chances are they'll have their own ideas for decorating it. If they want more privacy, have them grow a wall of runner beans.

Succulents are popular plants for collections. Arrange extravagant displays of them, and place them on a pedestal so people can see up close their pretty rosette shapes and subtle colors.

GLASS MULCHES and painted tree trunks create a magical otherworldly landscape. For information on how to keep glass clean, see page 80. For a source of crushed glass, try a local glass recycling plant. Design: Andy Cao.

MAKE YOUR FAVORITE plants and garden views look as pretty as a picture by framing them. Choose an antique picture frame, as shown here, or a discarded window frame from a house. Plant it in the ground (by attaching it to stakes), or hang it from a branch, or wedge it into a hole in a hedge. Design: Ivan Hicks.

A SMALL PATIO of Salmon Bay pebbles glitters with a waterfall of tumbled glass and pottery shards from Glass Beach, in northern California, where an old landfill has been eroded by the Pacific Ocean and pieces of glass have been tumbled by the waves. To tumble your own materials, look under Lapidary Equipment in the Yellow Pages. Design: Marcia Donahue.

ANTIQUE WINDOWS contribute color and sculptural presence to a winter landscape. Topped with ice or snow on a sunny morning, they would be all dazzle and sparkle. Design: Rick Darke.

OLD TILE and rusty furniture lend beautiful color and texture to this outdoor eating area in Janet Rademacker's garden in Arizona. The garden is a yard show of innovatively deployed found and recycled objects, such as metal containers, bedsprings, bottles, and tractor headlamps. Rademacker has made sculptures of some of the objects and hung them on the plain garden walls. Everywhere the eye rests, there is a story.

As you place "animals" in your garden, think about their habitat and needs. They'll assume more presence if you've conjured something of their natural world. This turtle (created by Claire Dohna) has tender leaves to nibble on and some shade and shelter; it's perhaps making its way toward water. Stranded atop a wall, it might be disconcerting.

This grand stone sofa, created by artist Donna Billick, is made grander by its placement: on a proscenium two steps above the path, with a soft carpet of dymondia sweeping up the path and around it. Design: Bob Clark.

To help children create their personal, eccentric worlds, provide a few boulders, sand, water, and movable objects such as leaves, pebbles, feathers, and teacups.

This lady needs some privacy, so she's been set amid tall foliage. She looks as if she wouldn't appreciate competition, which is perhaps why she wasn't placed among flowers. Her lipstick and hat are garden decoration enough, and you can't help wanting to catch the sunlight slipping down her back. Design: Sharon Osmond.

RAIN OR SHINE, trains chug along 500 feet of this Colorado track, past limestone cliffs, through meadows of sweet alyssum, over fields of Irish moss, under giant spruces that are 1 foot tall. Every landscape detail has been scaled to the trains. For more information on creating magical miniaturized landscapes, see page 81. Design: Tom Speer.

LINKS TO OTHER THEMES

Here are some ways to settle your personal, eccentric garden alongside a part of your garden with a different theme. For more information, see pages 4–13.

To link a personal, eccentric garden to a Mediterranean garden, use tile or shells in both. Alligators, flamingos, parrots, and other exotic elements are at home in a tropical garden as well as a personal, eccentric garden. To tie a personal, eccentric garden to a natural garden, use logs or tree stumps in both. Cherubs and other heavenly objects might be repeated in a sanctuary garden.

THESE CERAMIC GROTESQUES were bought as architectural salvage, left over from a restoration project at City College in New York. Set by a garden path, they startle and give you a thrill as you walk past their haunted eyes. The garden contains other thrill-provoking elements: cliffs, deep water, dark thickets, poisonous plants, and paths that go almost underground. Design: Roger Raiche, David McCrory.

Working with Rebar

The metal reinforcing bar used in concrete work is an adaptable material, well suited to creating arches or other plant supports, as well as garden sculpture. (This rebar "tree" was created by Tom Chakas.)

Rebar is sold in various thicknesses: select ⅜ inch, ½ inch, or ⅝ inch for garden projects. Pencil rod, which is only ¼ inch thick and lacks the ribbing of thicker rebar, can be bent by hand and is useful for smaller sculptures.

You can bend ⅜-inch rebar by standing on it and pulling, if you have enough strength. If that doesn't work or if you are using thicker rebar, rent or buy a set of rebar benders to hold the metal firmly and bend it as you wish. You can also set up a jig, such as a series of sturdy metal pipes driven into the ground; you pull the rebar around the jig to create curves.

Many suppliers of rebar will cut it to the lengths you need. Or you can cut it yourself with a hacksaw or a skill saw fitted with a metal-cutting blade.

To anchor a rebar sculpture or arch, pour concrete as you would for a post hole or pier; push the rebar in before the concrete sets completely, checking to make sure it is plumb. Alternatively, cap one end of a piece of metal or PVC pipe, and pound it (cap down) into soft ground. Then place the "foot" of the rebar piece into the pipe. If necessary, pack gravel into the pipe around the rebar to help keep the rebar plumb.

Displaying Stones

Many gardeners collect beautiful and unusual stones as passionately as they do plants. Creating an artful display for a trove of stones adds a distinctly personal touch to the garden. Try placing special stones as accents to plants growing in large containers. Use them to create a beach at the edge of a pond or to make a dry creek. Arrange stones in groups alongside a path or on top of a wall. Special stones make a pretty base for a spill fountain installed in a patio or courtyard.

Set bands of stones and pebbles in the soil to make a garden floor (the one shown here is based on a design by Jeff Bale).

You can drill holes through pebbles with pretty striations and colors and thread them on metal rods to form a sculpture or a low fence. Use a nut above and below to hold the stones in place.

Personalizing Concrete

Concrete doesn't have to be straight rectangular paving or plain, utilitarian gray. You can bring style and pizzazz to concrete by coloring it, sculpting it into interesting shapes, or adding surface patterns and decorations.

Color concrete by mixing specially made pigments with the cement in a dry state, or dusting on colors just after the cement has been poured and smoothed. There are several ways to stain or paint older concrete. Chemical stains for concrete create mottled colors that have a rich patina. Semitransparent wood stains also work well, as does exterior paint intended for concrete; apply two or three coats. When working with concrete, be sure to wear gloves and any other safety equipment specified on product labels. Follow label directions for mixing concrete.

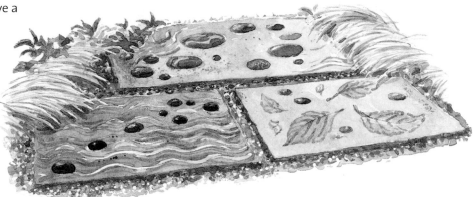

1. Concrete for paths is usually poured in forms. However, you can make free-form shapes, such as these giant stepping-stones (designed by Katzmaier Newell Kehr). Dig holes at least 4 inches deep, mix the concrete, and fill each hole; level the concrete. (Where the soil freezes, dig deeper holes, and lay 6 inches of gravel beneath the concrete.) The late Harland Hand, a California artist and garden designer, sculpted concrete not only into free-form stepping-stones but also into stairs, slabs for terraces, pools, and boulderlike shapes that serve as seats. He dumped wet, but stiff, concrete directly on the ground and troweled it into the irregular, granitelike shapes he favored. (For a photo of his work, see page 72.)

2. Smaller, movable stepping-stones are easy to make and fun to decorate. Build a form with a plywood bottom and 1-by-2 lumber for the sides. Apply a mold release agent or vegetable oil to all surfaces that will come in contact with the concrete. To provide texture, line the bottom of the form with burlap, bits of shell, tiles, or thin pieces of wood or bamboo; after the concrete sets, remove the paver from the form and turn it over to display the pattern. Alternatively, pour concrete into the form, and decorate by pressing leaves into the top, raking the surface, or incising designs while the concrete is damp.

3. Smooth river rock, small pebbles, bits of tile, or other found or salvaged objects can be set in wet concrete to make a pattern or mosaic design.

Pour the concrete as usual, but don't fill the forms or hole completely. Push the stones or other materials into the concrete one by one, sinking each slightly more than half. Press on them with a board to make them level. When the concrete has hardened somewhat, expose and clean the design by brushing the concrete while wetting the surface with a fine spray.

Exploring Color

Developing your sense of color and color preferences is an ongoing, personal process that evolves as your garden grows and changes. There are lots of ways to learn about color and how it affects you. Note which colors especially catch your attention in your own garden and in other people's gardens. Look at combinations of colors; when placed together, colors alter and affect each other. Background colors, such as a haze of green leaves or a gray fence,

HARMONIOUS COLORS

are important, but often overlooked, factors in our perception of color. What elements besides plants contribute color to the scene? Perhaps a bright blue chair or door is echoed by a pair of blue ceramic pots, bringing contrast to a nearby deep red rose. Or a rusty metal sculpture may be placed in front of a pinkish stucco wall that is

covered with a cream-flowered clematis vine. It's helpful to take notes or, better, take photographs or make colored sketches of colors and combinations that attract you. Keep a scrapbook of these ideas, adding paint chips and fabric swatches, too.

Many gardeners are attracted to boldly contrasting colors, such as violet and yellow or red and green. Others favor color schemes that feature closely related colors, such as violet and pink or chartreuse and yellow, which are less startling and more harmonious to the eye.

CONTRASTING COLORS

Keeping Glass Clean

Gardeners on the cutting edge are using recycled glass in the garden as mulch for small areas or as a topping for a path, as well as in and around water features. The pebblelike glass is made from bottles, crushed mechanically and tumbled to smooth the edges. Like gravel, this material collects fallen leaves and other debris. You can clean the surface by using a blower, spraying with a jet of water, raking gently, or sweeping with a soft-bristled broom or large brush.

Glass balls make interesting accents placed in a bowl or floating in a pond. These glass pieces also get grimy; to keep them sparkling, periodically scrub them with a brush in a container of soapy water. Rinse well.

Staging Plant Collections

Collections of plants have a way of getting out of hand. Every season there are tempting, even irresistible, offerings of new plants, all of which have to be fitted into the garden somehow. Several strategies can help you bring order to a collection of varied plants.

Repeating plants along a garden border sets up a rhythm that is pleasing to the eye; between the featured, repeated plants, set out a selection of diverse plants. Also consider grouping plants by color. For example, create a white garden, choosing plants that have white flowers, and maintain interest by varying the flower and leaf form, leaf color, and plant shape and size.

Staging plant collections in groups of containers is another way to avoid a hodgepodge look. To enhance cohesiveness, choose containers with similar surfaces, such as pots glazed in shades of blue and green or all terra-cotta pots. Set the pots in a line along a path, atop a wall, or on steps. Or create a focal point by placing them in tiers on an étagère, either purchased or homemade.

Manipulating Scale

Changing the scale or relative size of objects can help you create a magical world detached from ordinary reality. Here a fanciful castle, surrounded by a moat, has been set in a bed of fine-textured ground cover. The gardener might have chosen to continue the miniaturized theme by surrounding the castle with other small-leafed plants. Instead, the seemingly gigantic leaves of a hosta create a junglelike forest behind the castle, manipulating the scale of the scene. Boulders, chosen for their resemblance to mountains, make up the background; a (relatively) huge dragon lurks behind the mountains.

Place a scene like this in a hidden, secret spot, a place with a bit of mystery, such as in dappled shade off to one side of a narrow path. Separate it from places with a normal sense of scale.

Play with the elements, adding, subtracting, and rearranging them to see what works. For example, in this scene, you might decide to remove the dragon: perhaps it is actually too large, out of scale with the other objects, or perhaps it detracts from the simplicity of the overall picture. Keep in mind that this sort of scene is most dramatic when quite simple, with each detail serving a purpose.

Plants and Materials

Gardeners who cultivate personal, eccentric gardens are always on the lookout for a wide and interesting variety of plants. They often choose cultivars for their unusual colors and variations in foliage, as much as for their flowers. Plants may be selected for sheer drama, perhaps their arresting size, exceptional shape, or unique form. Collections of plants offer further intriguing possibilities. Such collections may feature numerous varieties of related plants, such as hostas, or a more personal, eclectic assemblage of plants that pique the gardener's interest at the moment. A few suggestions are given here to get you started. Except as noted, the plants described require full sun to partial shade, average, well-drained garden soil, regular watering, and fertilizer. Hardiness is given in parentheses.

Allium

With their rounded clusters of flowers atop tall leafless stalks, these ornamental relatives of the common onion make truly dramatic accents in the garden (−20°F/−29°C). Giant allium, *A. gigantium,* has spectacular softball-size clusters of lavender blossoms on 5- to 6-foot stalks in summer. Slightly smaller, spring-blooming *A. rosenbachianum* 'Album' has unusual greenish white blossoms.

Auricula *(Primula auricula)*

These special primroses are collected by connoisseurs and generally displayed in pots, though some kinds are good border plants (−20°F/−29°C). Evergreen plants 6 to 8 inches high, auriculas have clusters of fragrant springtime blooms in many colors. Especially choice varieties have green

Fill an old (or uncomfortable) pair of boots with variegated carpet bugle and violas for a touch of pathside whimsy.

or nearly black flowers rimmed in a mealy powder or in a contrasting color.

Carpet Bugle *(Ajuga reptans)*

Carpet bugle is popular as an evergreen ground cover (−40°F/−40°C) that spreads rapidly by runners. Some kinds have especially colorful foliage: 'Burgundy Lace' features reddish purple foliage splotched with white and pink; the leaves of 'Multicolor' are green blended with white and pinkish purple. Both grow about 4 inches high. 'Catlin's Giant' has extra-large (to 6 inches long) bronzy green leaves. These selections have spikes of blue flowers in spring.

Euphorbia

The euphorbias described here are perennials (−20°F/−29°C); there are also trees, shrubs, and succulents in this diverse group of plants. All have showy petallike bracts surrounding the small true flowers. The trailing stems of evergreen *E. myrsinites* radiate outward from the central crown. They are clothed in roundish, blue-gray leaves; chartreuse flowers appear in late winter. The purple foliage of *E. dulcis* 'Chameleon' emerges in spring, forming a 1-foot-high mound that's soon covered with bright yellow bracts.

Flowering Maple *(Abutilon* hybrids)

Reaching 8 to 10 feet tall and wide, these evergreen shrubs (20°F/−7°C) are prized for their drooping, bell-like flowers in white, yellow, pink, or red. The leaves resemble those of (unrelated) maples. Selections include 'Crimson Belle', with red flowers, and 'Kentish Belle', with yellow-orange ones. In cold-winter climates, grow flowering maples as annuals, or move them indoors in winter.

Gunnera *(G. tinctoria)*

Also known as "dinosaur food," gunneras (0°F/−18°C) are bold, even awe-inspiring, plants with giant, veined, lobed leaves, 4 to 8 feet across, on 4- to 6-foot stalks. Leaves and stems are covered with stiff hairs. New leaves appear each spring, though in mild climates old leaves stay green for more than a year. In colder areas, the foliage dies back in winter; protect the crowns with a thick mulch. Grow gunneras in rich, moist soil.

Hellebore *(Helleborus)*

Distinctive plants with handsome evergreen foliage, hellebores bear lovely roselike blossoms. Bear's-foot hellebore, *H. foetidus* (−10°F/−23°C), features dark green foliage on 1½-foot stems and, in spring, clusters of green blossoms with purple markings. Lenten rose, *H. orientalis* (−20°F/−29°C), also about 1½ feet tall, has nodding, often spotted flowers (white, greenish white, pink, maroon, or purple) that brighten the garden in early spring. Hellebores grow best in shade.

Hosta

Hostas (−40°F/−40°C) are a plant collector's dream. They are available in a huge assortment of cultivars and species with exceptionally attractive foliage; the spikes of pastel flowers in spring or summer are a bonus. Leaves may be lance-shaped, heart-shaped, oval, or round, with smooth or puckered surfaces. Leaf color ranges from light green to dark green, chartreuse, near yellow, and almost blue; many species are variegated. Hostas form a mound of foliage ranging in size from a few inches to 3 to 4 feet high and wide. Plant them in a shady spot.

Phormium

Bold plants for garden beds and containers, these striking evergreens (20°F/−7°C) form clumps of sword-shaped leaves. There is a considerable choice of plant size and foliage color. *P. tenax* 'Jack Spratt' grows only 1½ feet tall and wide, with twisting, reddish brown leaves, while *P. t.* 'Variegatum', with grayish green leaves edged in cream, can reach 8 feet tall. Hybrid 'Apricot Queen' forms a dense 3-foot-tall clump of yellowish green, apricot-blushed leaves with a thin red margin.

Sedge *(Carex)*

Grasslike sedge plants are effective in borders, in containers, and near water features. Evergreen leatherleaf sedge, *C. buchananii* (−20°F/−29°C), forms a 2- to 3-foot clump of curly-tipped, reddish bronze leaves. Bowles' golden sedge, *C. elata* 'Aurea' (−30°F/−34°C), grows about 2½ feet tall. The narrow leaves emerge bright yellow in spring, becoming green in late summer; it needs ample moisture.

Stone Plant

Offering fascinating possibilities for plant collections, stone plants (also known as living rocks) are amazing replicas of pebbles. Native to dry areas of South Africa, they grow as rounded forms low on the ground. A number of genera contain stone plants. One of the most popular is *Lithops* (50°F/10°C). Shaped like inverted cones, most lithops grow 2 to 4 inches high; leaves and a single stemless flower emerge from a central fissure. Grow stone plants in containers of fast-draining mix. They need little water.

Succulents

An amazing variety of colors and shapes in both foliage and flowers give succulents a strong impact massed in the garden or showcased in containers. Striking, shrubby *Aeonium arboreum* 'Zwartkop' (32°F/0°C) grows to 3 feet tall and wide. Branches end in 6- to 8-inch rosettes of shiny, fleshy, almost-black leaves; long clusters of yellow flowers appear in summer. *Echeveria* hybrids (32°F/0°C) feature low-growing rosettes of fancy leaves, some crimped, some waved; leaf colors include lavender-blue, bronze, and purple.

Sedum species may be trailing or large and upright. For a hanging basket, choose donkey tail, *S. morganianum* (32°F/0°C). Its fleshy green leaves on trailing stems can grow 4 feet long. Some cultivars of *S. telephium* (−25°F/−32°C) offer colorful foliage plus clusters of late-summer flowers on 2-foot-tall plants. 'Arthur Branch' has purplish bronze leaves and deep pink flowers; pink-flowered 'Matrona' has red-blushed foliage with pink edges. Succulents are drought tolerant and easy to grow; bring tender ones indoors in winter.

Finding Salvage Materials

Salvage and recycled materials—from old wooden chairs to used bowling balls to manhole covers (reincarnated as pavers)—can be decorative in gardens. (This divider is in Nancy Goldman's garden.) To find salvage objects, check the Yellow Pages under headings such as Architectural Salvage; Building Materials—Architectural, Antique, and Used; and Salvage Merchandise. Garage sales, antique stores, and used furniture stores are also good bets.

Purchasing Garden Art

Art for your garden may be anything from arrangements of salvage objects to colorful ceramics to large murals and sculptures. (The piece shown here is by Sue Skelly.) Artists' open studios, gallery exhibits, and shows at community art centers and art colleges showcase artists, offering a wealth of ideas and objects. At these venues you may find an artist (or student) whose work you admire and whom you can commission to produce art designed especially for your garden. It's a good idea to specify in a written contract the commission details on payment, delivery dates, and installation.

Tropical Gardens

A tropical garden teems with bold, exuberant foliage that creeps along the garden floor and rises to the treetops. The look is lush and richly green, but the giant leaves of the undergrowth are often striped, ribbed, or flushed with bright color. Tropical flowers are usually striking in color, too; many have trumpet blossoms; some emit heavy scents at night.

Design, left: Raymond Jungles.

MANY DESIGNERS choose dark-foliaged tropicals, such as tall 'Black Magic' elephant's ear (*Colocasia*) and trailing sweet potato *Ipomoea batatas* 'Blackie', because they intensify the bright colors of neighboring plants, such as the coleus 'Sunrise' here.

THIS TROPICAL WALK at Chanticleer Garden in Pennsylvania *(below)* shows the bold, coarse-textured foliage that is the hallmark of a tropical garden. The spiky focal point at the path corner is Adam's needle (*Yucca filamentosa* 'Bright Edge'). Behind it are a tall purple coleus hedge, banana (*Musa* species), castor bean (*Ricinus communis*), and elephant's ear (*Colocasia esculenta*). The giant leaves at the left of the path belong to rice paper plant *(Tetrapanax papyriferus)*. In the foreground are scarlet bromeliads *(Guzmania lingulata cardinalis)*. Note the absence of flowers.

To give tropical texture to a garden, contrast tall, upright, large-leafed plants such as canna with smaller or softer-looking ones like honey bush (*Melianthus major*) and fine foliage such as ornamental grasses.

If you have any of the following already
in your garden, use it as a starting point
for a tropical garden:

- palm tree
- tree canopy
- jungle of vines
- ferns
- pond or swimming pool
- lanai or porch
- large pots
- garden umbrella or hammock

A tropical garden is an excellent choice
for a container garden or a pool- or
pond-side garden.

A BLUE WALL helps make a tropical
effect with *Canna* 'Tropicanna',
Catalpa bignonioides 'Aurea', and
Miscanthus sinensis 'Variegatus' in a
garden in the Northwest (blue is at
the opposite side of the color wheel
from orange, so together they sizzle
with contrast). Design: Linda
Cochran.

CANNAS ARE TROPICAL favorites because of their brilliantly colored paddle-
shaped leaves and showy hot flowers. For a supercolorful tropical bed,
match them with a coleus *(above)*, choosing varieties of canna and coleus
that share the same shades of pink and gold, or burgundy and lime, or
orange and red—both plants come in innumerable color combinations.
Alternatively, draw attention to the midribs and veins of canna leaves by
growing them alongside an elephant's ear such as *Alocasia macrorrhiza*
(right) with its awesome leaf structure.

SOME PALMS, like cabada palm *(Dypsis cabadae)*, are tall and feathery and are best planted in groups *(left)*. Others, such as sago palm *(Cycas revoluta,* not a true palm), are stocky and full; a single one serves well as an accent *(right)*. Sago palms are slow-growing; in a cold climate, grow them in containers so that in winter you can take them indoors as houseplants. For more information on palms, see page 97. Design, left: Raymond Jungles. Design, right: Landcraft Environments.

THIS FRONT PORCH in northern California was formerly a drab concrete slab. To create a lush tropical garden in a small space, choose fine-textured plants such as maidenhair ferns and feathery palms; they make the space look larger. The Balinese temple umbrella is both decorative and functional—it protects the plants from the noonday sun. Design: Davis Dalbok.

THIS TROPICAL water garden, flanked by bromeliads, decorates an entry in Kaneohe, Hawaii. To make your own, choose a small water lily and a large container. Consider a fragrant tropical water lily that opens at night. (For information on planting a water garden, see page 93.)

TROPICAL GARDENS have an oversize scale. This bowl is waist high; the reflections, so close, stop you in your tracks, and then you notice the details of the undersides of the giant banana leaves and gaze up to find the large pot of vining nasturtiums and love-lies-bleeding (*Amaranthus caudatus*) placed atop a very tall column. Design: Little and Lewis.

For a lush tropical pond, plunge pots of papyrus or umbrella plant (*Cyperus* species), cannas (most are suitable), and tropical water lilies into the water. Float water hyacinth on the water surface.

BRIGHT, GLISTENING TILE puts a tropical look on this garden wall in Key West, Florida; shadows and reflections of the foliage play on the wall and the water. If you garden in a dry region, consider tile and a fountain or small pond to evoke a sense of tropical color and moisture. Design: Debra Yates, Raymond Jungles.

THE FLOWERS of ginger lily (*Hedychium* species) have a heavy tropical fragrance; white ginger flowers are used in leis in Hawaii. Frost will kill the plants to the ground, but new stalks appear in early spring. Plant one in a large container, and place it in light shade near a seat. Other highly fragrant plants common in tropical gardens include angel's trumpet (*Brugmansia*), night jessamine (*Cestrum nocturnum*), and gardenia.

To create an old-fashioned tropical flowerbed in a lawn, make a mound, and plant it with pampas grass, canna, coleus, and dusty miller *(Centaurea cineraria).* For a modern look, mark out a series of rectangles, and plant each with one low-growing tropical plant; choose bold contrasting foliage colors and shapes.

IN NATURE, epiphytic orchids cling to the high branches of trees in tropical or subtropical jungles. For information on growing epiphytes in your garden, see page 95. This is a cattleya brassavola hybrid.

Here are some ways to settle your tropical garden alongside a part of your garden with a different theme. For more information, see pages 4–13.

To link a tropical garden to a Mediterranean garden or a personal, eccentric garden, use tile in both. To tie a tropical garden to a Japanese garden, plant delicate or large ferns in both. Hot-colored annuals such as petunias and passionflower vines suit a cottage garden and a tropical one. Plant fragrant jasmine in a sanctuary garden adjoining a tropical garden.

THIS PATH in an Oregon garden becomes a tropical corridor every summer. In winter, you can lift the elephant's ear (*Colocasia*) tubers from the pots and bring them indoors or move the pots to a sheltered spot. Coleus and impatiens can be started fresh each season. Note the delicate tropical-looking tree canopy overhead and the contrast of leaf textures so common in tropical gardens. For more information on overwintering tropicals, see page 95. Design: Ron Wagner, Nani Waddoups.

NOT TOO LONG AGO, this garden was a scruffy lawn bordered by a chain-link fence. First tropical trees were planted to create a forest canopy; then understory plants such as bromeliads and ferns were placed beneath them and epiphytes were attached to the trees. Ground covers were planted on the garden floor. To achieve a sense of age, paths were made of old foundation stones, and landscape boulders were placed at the path edge, where vegetation was allowed to engulf them. For more information on planning the layers of a jungle, see page 92. Design: Leland Miyano.

Planning a Jungle

The key feature of a tropical garden is interwoven layers of lush-looking plants: a green ceiling or canopy of trees; a middle layer of tall shrubs, many boasting oversize leaves, plus a few hanging baskets; and a floor alive with colored foliage and bright flowers. Vines weave exuberantly through all the layers, tying them together.

To plan a jungle, start with the canopy—the trees that shelter and shade the garden, at the same time giving it a sense of age and permanence. In a mild climate, the canopy might consist of tall palms, swaying in the breeze, and huge Florida figs (*Ficus rubiginosa*). In colder climates, deciduous trees with fine-textured leaves and spreading branches work well, such as silk tree (*Albizia julibrissin*) and honey locust (*Gleditsia triacanthos*). Almost any tree that forms a jungle canopy benefits from thinning—removing a few branches to let light into the lower layers of the garden. Though a tropical forest may be somewhat shady, it won't be welcoming to people or to other plants if it is too dark.

Below the canopy, plan for shrubs that are or look tropical. You might include some with huge leaves, such as bananas or cannas; for the contrast in leaf size and shape that characterizes a true jungle, set out large ferns and ornamental grasses. Hanging baskets filled with colorful coleuses and drooping vines, such as sweet potato vine (*Ipomoea batatas*), add to the complexity of the middle layer, as do epiphytes growing on tree trunks at eye level.

The jungle floor is home to dense groups of shorter plants. Look for bromeliads, caladiums, and coleuses with wonderfully colored foliage, as well as flowering plants such as impatiens and fuchsias. Again, contrasting foliage is important; include small ferns and narrow-leafed plants such as grasses or sedges.

Vines, twining and tumbling through the layers of plants, make the jungle truly convincing. They can be fast-growing tender vines such as jasmine and bougainvillea (overwinter indoors in cold regions), hardier sorts such as fiveleaf akebia (*Akebia quinata*) or Dutchman's pipe (*Aristolochia durior*), or annuals such as moonflower (*Ipomoea alba*).

Creating an Instant Tropical Water Garden

For a quick tropical touch, set up a water garden in a large container, and fill it with lush, fast-growing plants. Shown here are a dramatic canna, blue flag iris *(Iris versicolor)*, and, twisting over the edges, corkscrew rush *(Juncus effusus* 'Spiralis'). Select a large glazed container without a drainage hole, and move it to its permanent position—once filled with water it will be very heavy.

1. Cover the soil in each plant's pot with a ½-inch layer of pebbles to keep the soil in place. Arrange the plants in the water garden container, placing the largest in the center or at the back. Bring smaller plants to the correct height by setting them on overturned pots or on bricks. Most aquatic plants do best with an inch or more of water over the crown.

2. Use a carpenter's level to check that the rim of the container is level; then fill the container with water. Add a mosquito-control ring; available at nurseries, these rings contain a naturally occurring bacterium that kills mosquito larvae. Check the water level regularly, and add water as needed. Feed the plants with an aquatic plant fertilizer, following directions on the label.

Planting Lavish Tropical Pots

A densely planted big pot—or two or three—brings the sizzle of the topics to your garden, whether displayed on your deck or patio or set right in a garden bed. Put large pots in their permanent locations before planting, since they will be heavy once filled with soil. When choosing plants, start with a substantial anchor plant for the center, such as a canna or hibiscus. Fill in with smaller tropical-looking plants, such as brightly colored coleuses and impatiens, and soften the edges with trailing variegated ivy or sweet potato vine.

To plant, fill the pot a little more than halfway with potting mix. Mix in controlled-release fertilizer in the amount directed on the package. Remove the large plant from its nursery container; center it in the pot. Place more mix under its roots, if needed, so that the top of the root ball will rest about 2 inches below the pot rim. Add more mix, and set in the smaller plants; firm potting mix around all of the root balls. Water thoroughly after planting and as often as needed to keep the potting mix damp. Give supplemental feedings of liquid fertilizer each month.

Hanging a Hammock

For a relaxing view of your jungle canopy, stretch out on a hammock, and take in the branches swaying in the breeze, the cries of birds, and the scents of flowers. (This one is hung in a garden designed by Margaret West.) You can choose a classic hammock made of natural cotton rope, one using synthetic rope (which is more resistant to mildew and weather), a cloth hammock, a soft quilted or padded style, or a hammock chair.

Whichever sort appeals to you, be sure to hang it securely. Two strong trees or posts, about 12 to 15 feet apart, provide an ideal site for a hammock. To protect the tree bark, put padding under encircling ropes, or use specially made tree-friendly nylon straps. Insert sturdy threaded hooks to hang a hammock from posts; the posts should be set in concrete. You can also suspend a hammock or hammock chair from the beams of an overhead structure. Or buy a freestanding hammock, with a frame made of metal or wood; some of these have wheels, which make it easy for one person to move the hammock.

Planting a Pineapple

A member of the bromeliad family, the pineapple may be the ultimate tropical fruit. You can grow pineapples in pots, kept outdoors year-round in climates where temperatures stay above 60°F/16°C; bring the pots indoors for winter in colder regions, or grow the plants year-round in a greenhouse. The process is not difficult, but it does call for patience—plants can take up to 24 months to produce ripe fruit.

1. Buy a supermarket pineapple with healthy green leaves. Cut off the crown, leaving 1 to 2 inches of fruit. Allow the crown to dry in a shady spot for several days.

2. Choose a 1-gallon plastic pot with a drainage hole. Fill it about ¾ full with lava rock. Add 2 to 3 inches of redwood compost or potting mix formulated for orchids.

3. Set the crown on top of the compost, and add a little more compost around its base. Place the pot in a warm, sunny location, and water frequently. When new leaves begin to grow, start fertilizing. Use a dry fertilizer meant for citrus every three to four months; also mix liquid fertilizer into the irrigation water once a month. When the pineapple outgrows its original container, transplant it, first to a 5-gallon pot filled with rich compost and then to a 15-gallon pot.

Growing Epiphytes

In a tropical forest, every habitat is home to some sort of plant. Epiphytes are among the most opportunistic, attaching themselves to tree trunks or branches, in reach of rainwater and light. Unlike parasites, which draw nourishment from the host plant, epiphytes live on nutrients drawn from air, rainwater, and organic debris on the supporting plant. You can mount some epiphytes on pieces of wood, such as cedar, juniper, oak, or grape, or slabs of tree fern. In summer, fasten the mounted epiphytes to outdoor trees or arbors for a junglelike effect. In cold climates, bring them indoors in winter; if your garden is frost free, you can grow epiphytes directly on trees.

Exotic-looking tillandsias (a type of bromeliad also known as air plant), shown here, are easy to mount. Select a piece of wood for the mount and several young tillandsias. Trim back long roots, leaving some to attach. Apply hot glue or another nontoxic adhesive to the mount (let hot glue cool for a few seconds afterward). Press the roots against the adhesive. Take care not to get glue on the tender base of the plant. Hold the plant in place until the glue has set, or secure the plant temporarily with twine or wire.

You can also mount other kinds of epiphytic bromeliads, staghorn fern *(Platycerium bifurcatum),* and some orchids; these plants generally have a larger root system, so you need to tie a ball of damp sphagnum moss around the roots before fastening them to the wood with nylon thread.

Keep the mounted plants in a partially shaded spot with good air circulation (indoors or out), and mist them with water daily in summer, weekly in winter.

Overwintering Tubers and Rhizomes

Some favorite tropical plants grow from tubers or rhizomes, which, like bulbs, are storage organs, holding reserves of food that keep the plant alive from one growing season to the next. Tubers and rhizomes native to tropical regions cannot survive outdoors in winter where the soil freezes, so dig them up in the fall, and store them in a cool, frost-free place until the next spring. Caladium, canna, elephant's ear *(Colocasia esculenta* and *Alocasia macrorrhiza),* and sweet potato vine *(Ipomoea batatas)* need this overwintering.

1. In fall, around the time of the first frost, cut back the stems, and dig the tubers or rhizomes from the ground or knock them out of their containers. Remove the leaves and soil; then spread the tubers or rhizomes on a screen or on newspapers in a shaded, frost-free location, and let them dry for several days. Be sure to keep a label with each kind, so you'll know what you have, come spring.

2. Once they are dry, place them in a single layer in a box that has a lid, making sure they don't touch one another (separation lessens the chance of any decay spreading from one to another). Cover them with dry sand, sawdust, perlite, or peat moss. Cover the box, and store it in a cool, dry place (35° to 55°F/2° to 13°C).

3. To get a jump start on the growing season, pot the tubers and rhizomes in early spring. Bring them into a sunny room, where they will begin to grow much sooner than they would if you waited until the weather warms enough to plant them directly outdoors.

Plants and Materials

Big, bold, lush, and *colorful* are words that only begin to describe plants for tropical gardens. Many are grown not for their flowers but for their foliage, featuring huge, shiny, compound, or textured leaves that enliven the garden for many months. Tropical plants grown for flowers are bold, too, with exotic shapes or dazzling colors. Except as noted, the plants described here grow best in full sun to partial shade in rich, moist soil, with regular feeding. Hardiness is noted in parentheses; many are sensitive to frost, so suggestions are given for protecting them over the winter in cold climates.

Banana

Bananas in gardens are grown for their spectacular leaves, rather than their fruit. Hardiest is Japanese banana, *Musa basjoo* (foliage freezes at 28°F/–2°C, roots survive to 0°F/–18°C or lower if mulched). It can reach 15 feet high, with narrow green leaves to 8 feet long and exotic yellow flowers. Red Abyssinian banana, *Ensete ventricosum* 'Maurelii', grows to 20 feet high, with reddish leaves as long as 15 feet (foliage freezes at about 30°F/–1°C, roots survive to 20°F/–7°C or lower if mulched). If you grow bananas in containers, cut back the stems and store the plants indoors in winter.

Bromeliad

This large family of showy plants includes epiphytic tillandsias and edible pineapple, as well as a host of relatives. All feature rosettes of handsome, straplike leaves with a water-holding "cup" in the center and dramatic flower heads. Often grown as choice houseplants, bromeliads such as guzmanias and vrieseas can summer outdoors in a partially shaded location (hardy to 40°F/4°C). Display them potted singly or combined with other tropical plants in a large container. Irrigate by pouring water directly into the cup, allowing the excess to spill out and moisten the soil below. Move them indoors in winter.

Caladium *(C. bicolor)*

Caladiums grow 2 feet tall and produce arrow-shaped leaves as long as 1½ feet, colored in bands and speckles of red, pink, green, silver, bronze, and white. To look their best, they need high humidity and hot weather (hardy to only 55°F/13°C). Most require a shady location, but some newer varieties, such as 'Fire Chief' and 'Rose Bud' tolerate more sun. Store tubers indoors in winter (see page 95).

Canna

Flaunting spikes of big, showy, irregularly shaped flowers and large leaves, cannas are easy to grow. Selections include 'Pretoria', a 6-footer with hot orange flowers and green leaves striped in gold, and 4-foot 'Red King Humbert', which features orange-red flowers and reddish bronze foliage. Cannas perform best in full sun. Planted in containers, most can be submerged in water gardens (see page 93). In the colder parts of their range, protect the rhizomes over winter with a 6-inch layer of mulch. Beyond their hardiness limit (10°F/–12°C), dig up and store the rhizomes (see page 95).

Coleus *(C. × hybridus)*

Valued for its dazzling foliage, coleus forms a bushy plant 1 to 3 feet high. The leaves vary from 1 to 7 inches long and may be toothed or ruffled; in most selections, each leaf displays two or more colors, with contrasting edges, splotches, and veins. The blue flower spikes are usually pinched out to make the plant more rounded. Most selections of this annual plant grow best in partial shade, but some newer cultivars take more sun.

Elephant's Ear
(Colocasia esculenta; Alocasia macrorrhiza)

One of the most magnificent plants for tropical gardens, *C. esculenta,* also called taro, boasts leathery, heart-shaped enormous leaves—to 2½ by 3 feet. Depending on the variety, the leaves may be solid green, green marked with purple, or solid purple. Handsome in large containers, this plant can also be grown submerged in a pond. The closely related *A. macrorrhiza* features huge, bright green, arrow-shaped leaves, 2 feet long or more. This species, also known as giant taro, is not suited to water gardens. In regions beyond their hardiness (20°F/–7°C), dig up and store the tubers of both species over winter (see page 95).

The large, deeply colored foliage of 6- to 10-foot-tall bloodleaf banana, Musa acuminate *'Sumatra' (hardy to 32°F/0°C), casts a tropical spell over the garden.*

Palm

With their elegant, feather-cut or fan-shaped fronds rattling in the wind, palms epitomize the tropics. While some palms achieve immense height, smaller ones are suited to garden culture, and some even thrive in containers. Young palms appreciate partial shade; however, most can take full sun when mature. Perhaps the hardiest of the family, needle palm, *Rhapidophyllum hystrix* (0°F/−18°C or lower), grows slowly to 8 feet high and wide, with dramatic fans of lustrous, dark green, 3-foot-wide leaves; it is shrubby, lacking a distinct trunk. Dwarf palmetto, *Sabal minor* (20°F/−7°C), grows only 3 to 6 feet tall and 10 feet wide, with a very short trunk and long, fan-shaped blue-green leaves. Windmill palm, *Trachycarpus fortunei* (10°F/−12°C or lower), reaches 30 feet high and 10 feet wide. Its trunk, which is usually thicker at the top than the bottom, is crowned with fan-shaped dark green leaves. If grown in containers, these palms can be moved indoors or to a cool greenhouse in winter.

Impatiens

Summer-blooming annuals, impatiens are versatile plants for tropical gardens, at home in hanging baskets, containers, and lightly shaded beds. Flowers are available in a wide range of brilliant and soft colors. Busy Lizzie (*I. walleriana*) includes plants from dwarf 6- to 12-inchers to 2-foot-tall strains; all have glossy green leaves and rounded flowers. New Guinea hybrid impatiens are striking plants to 2 feet high; their leaves are often variegated with cream or red.

Jasmine (*Jasminum*)

Jasmines provide sweetly perfumed white blossoms on vines that obligingly climb fences or arbors or spill from hanging baskets. Common white (or poet's) jasmine, *J. officinale*, and Spanish jasmine, *J. o. grandiflorum* (both 20°F/−7°C), bloom profusely in summer. Spanish jasmine can reach 15 feet, while common jasmine attains twice that size. In colder regions, grow jasmine in a container and move it indoors for winter.

Orchid

The immense orchid family offers opportunities to introduce truly exotic flowers to your tropical paradise. Several easier-to-grow sorts can summer outdoors, under the shade of high-branching trees or in an arbor, and come indoors for winter. These include *Cymbidium*, *Epidendrum*, and slipper orchids, *Paphiopedilum* (all are damaged at 28°F/−2°C). Consult local growers to find varieties for your region. Plant orchids in containers, using a planting mix made for orchids.

Sweet Potato Vine
(*Ipomoea batatas*)

A trailing tropical with heart-shaped or lobed leaves, sweet potato vine is attractive in hanging baskets and large pots. 'Blackie' has deep blackish purple leaves, while the chartreuse foliage of 'Marguerite' glows in the sun. 'Tricolor' (also called 'Pink Frost') features silvery green leaves streaked with pink and white. In cold climates (below 20°F/−7°C), dig up and store the tubers over winter (see page 95).

Tropical Hibiscus (*H. rosa-sinensis*)

A flamboyant flowering tropical shrub, hibiscus (30°F/−1°C) blooms all summer, producing huge (4 to 8 inches across) single or double flowers in every shade except blue. A popular houseplant, tropical hibiscus is also easy to grow in a sunny spot outdoors, in a container or in the ground. Shelter the plants indoors in winter in cold climates, or treat them as annuals.

Buying Fish

Besides contributing bright flashes of color to a pond, fish are useful in controlling mosquito larvae. Ordinary goldfish are well adapted to most sorts of water gardens. Koi, however, require a good-size pond that is at least 18 inches deep. Select fish with bright, clear eyes and erect fins. To acclimate the fish before releasing them from their plastic bag, float the bag on the water for about 20 minutes, keeping it shaded from the sun.

Choosing Tile

Bright, shiny tiles are delightful accents for a tropical garden. Glass and glazed ceramic tiles manufactured for outdoor use can be fashioned into exotic murals or water features. Most glass and glazed tiles are slippery when wet, making them unsafe for an entire walkway or terrace; however, they can serve as wonderful color accents interspersed among other paving materials.

Cottage Gardens

A cottage garden foams with old-fashioned flowers such

as sweet peas, hollyhocks, foxgloves, and daisies. They

all seem to have sprung up naturally, seeding themselves

joyously through the flowerbed—and sometimes out into

the path. Not one of them is prim; they lean casually,

or they flop tousled through one another in a vibrant

mingling. Fragrance is part of the cottage garden

romance, especially the fragrance of old roses.

Design, left: Karen Burroughs.

AN EXUBERANT old-fashioned-looking rose *(left)* is a hallmark of cottage gardens. Grow one on an arch to frame a view, train others over the house doors and windows, and let one or two run free in your flowerbeds or up a tree. This rose is 'Crimson Rambler', a vigorous, spring-flowering multiflora rambler. For more rose ideas, see pages 108 and 111. For a different, intensely fragrant, quintessential cottage climber, consider honeysuckle *(below)*.

THE EARLIEST COTTAGE gardens weren't a tumble of flowers. They were practical plots of vegetables, fruits, and herbs. For an authentic cottage garden, plant a few vegetables and scented herbs, such as mint and chives, among your flowers (see page 106).

To grow a rose through a tree canopy, plant it a few feet from the tree trunk, tip the canes to the trunk, using stakes to support them if necessary, and secure them with twine looped around the tree. Remove the climbing aids as soon as the rose gets a hold among the tree branches.

If you have any of the following already in your garden, use it as a starting point for a cottage garden:

- old-fashioned flowers
- self-seeding flowers
- old roses
- vegetable or herb garden
- twig trellis or plant supports
- picket or post-and-rail fence
- rustic garden structure

A cottage garden is an excellent choice for a casually maintained area of the garden or a cut-flower, vegetable, or herb garden. Children may enjoy growing cottage garden annuals from seed.

To CREATE AN UNPLANNED cottage garden effect, choose plants, such as this sweet pea *(above)*, that twine or seed themselves through other plants and produce small flowers in mixed colors, so dots of purple, pink, white, and red pop up everywhere. A garden with little or no mingling of colors *(below)* seems less spontaneous, more elegant. For more information on combining plants effectively, see page 107. Design, below: Joanna Reed.

THE CLASSIC PICKET FENCE is about 3 feet high; it marks a boundary, keeps animals out, and invites people to look in. Painting the pickets white *(above)* makes the fence look somewhat formal. A more rustic cottage garden look comes from leaving the fence unpainted *(below)*. A post-and-rail fence (see page 99, top right) is the most casual option. For more information on picket fences, see page 109. Design, above: Conni Cross.

CHOOSE A SIMPLE brick pattern for a cottage garden, and, if you have a choice, buy old bricks rather than new ones, because they are a gentler color and have nicely pitted surfaces and edges. Pink flowers suit the color of old brick; for new brick, look to soft warm reds, and let moss grow in the cracks to hide the sharp brick edges. Gravel, decomposed granite, and blue shale also make lovely cottage garden paths. Design: Wendy Witherick.

FLOWERS AND FOLIAGE spilling over the path are an essential feature of a cottage garden. Lady's-mantle (*Alchemilla mollis*), with its chartreuse summer flowers, spills beautifully and also seeds itself along the path; after a shower, you'll find the scallop-edged leaves full of raindrops. A narrow path is more charming to the eye than a path 4 feet wide, but you won't be able to stroll side by side with a friend, and if you walk it on a dewy morning you'll get your ankles wet.

To design a storybook cottage garden, run a straight path, preferably gravel, from a picket gate directly to the house door, and plant on either side of it.

IF STONE IS a local material used in buildings and walls in the neighborhood, it will look casual enough for a cottage garden, but don't bring in imported stone, especially the colorful kind. Choose large rectangles of cut stone; they look plainer and therefore more natural in a cottage garden than irregular stone pieces. The traditional cottage garden path is straight; the simple lines accentuate the loose naturalness of the flowers.

THE MOST BEAUTIFUL cottage garden decorations are usually practical, like this well-crafted twig trellis for sweet peas *(left)* and log-post arbor for a 'Goldbusch' rose *(below)*. Materials collected from the garden have an individual rustic character to them that no new materials can match. See page 109 for more ideas on how to use tree prunings.

A gate creates a moment of pause, a chance to leave your thoughts behind before you enter the garden. Make a cottage garden gate of simple materials; keep it low and open-structured so that it's welcoming; and choose an old-fashioned latch with a pretty-sounding click.

Here are some ways to settle your cottage garden alongside a part of your garden with a different theme. For more information, see pages 4–13.

Because cottage gardens are filled with flowers, a good linking strategy is to identify flowers that work effectively for both gardens. Lavenders, a mainstay of a Mediterranean garden, also work well in cottage gardens. Wildflowers can link a cottage garden to a natural one. Choose bright, hot-colored flowers for the border with a tropical garden, perhaps a few white or green flowers or foliage plants for the transition to a Japanese garden. Roses are an excellent cottage garden linking plant, too—have a fragrant one tumble over the threshold into a sanctuary garden, or let an informal cottage border with roses and lavenders morph into a formal rose garden with a lavender edging.

As an afternoon of weeding passes slowly into evening and you've lost all track of schedules and obligations, it's a pleasure to read the time from a shadow creeping over a flat stone. Place a sundial in an open sunny area. Practice leaving your watch indoors and living by the more natural-feeling time of the sun's passage across the sky.

Some benches prove more inviting than others. Choose one that's comfortable, and place it in a sheltered spot with at least some privacy and a lovely view out over the garden. An elegant bench (left) suits a spot close to the house, but a simple bench (right) is less intimidating. Design, right: Margaret de Haas van Dorsser.

Planting Vegetables, Fruits, and Herbs with Flowers

Originally, cottage gardens were planted primarily for sustenance; they included a wide variety of fruits, vegetables, and herbs and only a few flowers. Though the focus has gradually changed to favor ornamentals, planting edibles here and there adds to the old-fashioned charm of a cottage garden.

An apple, peach, pear, or other fruit tree brings a froth of springtime flowers followed by delicious fruit. For a true cottage garden look, set out flowering bulbs and annuals beneath the branches. For cottage gardens with limited space, a wide selection of dwarf fruit trees is available. To introduce fruit on a smaller scale, include blueberries in a border, or edge a flowerbed with strawberries.

Especially attractive vegetables include scarlet runner beans (plant them to climb a fence, where they'll produce clusters of vivid scarlet flowers and dark green beans), Swiss chard (select varieties with colored leafstalks, such as 'Rhubarb' and 'Bright Lights'), and kale ('Toscano' has dramatic dark, blistered, strap-shaped leaves). Basil, chives, dill, marjoram, oregano, and parsley are all pretty as well as tasty herb additions to a cottage garden. For a larger herb accent, plant 5-foot-tall fennel. The common variety features feathery green leaves. Bronze fennel ('Purpurascens', 'Smokey') is showier, with foliage of a soft, bronzy purple.

Planting a Chamomile Lawn

With its finely cut, aromatic, bright green leaves, chamomile can be used for a small-scale lawn that sets off nearby flowers perfectly. It's a tough, spreading plant that tolerates some foot traffic, although it's not suited to heavy traffic areas. And chamomile is easier to maintain than lawn grasses, requiring less water and little or no mowing. The most common type, *Chamaemelum nobile* (hardy to −10°F/−23°C), grows to 12 inches high, with small, buttonlike yellow flowers; in some forms, the blossoms resemble little white daisies. 'Treneague' is a nonblooming variety that grows only 3 inches high and does not need mowing. Chamomile is sold in flats at nurseries. (Fragrant, sweet chamomile tea comes from a different plant, the dried flowers of *Matricaria recutita*; this annual herb is right at home in cottage garden borders.)

1. Prepare a planting bed by removing existing plants and loosening the soil with a spading fork. Spread a 3- to 4-inch layer of organic matter (compost or nitrogen-fortified wood by-products, such as ground bark and sawdust) over the loosened soil. Use a spading fork to incorporate the organic matter evenly. Then level the bed with a rake, and water well.

2. With a sharp knife, cut across the flat of chamomile plants, making 2-inch-square plugs. Plant the plugs 6 to 12 inches apart. The closer spacing will fill in more quickly, but you'll need more plugs. Water often enough to keep the soil moist but not soggy. Once chamomile is established and growing well, it needs only moderate water.

Designing Plant Combinations

The hallmark of a cottage garden is an abundant and exuberant array of plants, full of color and fragrance and life. How do gardeners go about creating such a garden? There are no hard-and-fast rules—that's one reason cottage gardens are so much fun—but a few elements and ideas are important.

The color of flowers and foliage is one such element, and usually the most striking. You can plant a riot of colors for a truly joyous, wild effect. Or you may be a bit more structured and plant flowers In your favorite colors, perhaps a medley of bright tones, such as orange and gold accented with purple, or a softer combination of blue and white. Foliage color, though more subtle, adds interest and variety over a longer season than flower color. Besides a wide range of greens, you'll find plants with foliage in gray, silver, blue, chartreuse, yellow, bronze, and purple, as well as variegated plants, whose leaves combine two or three colors.

Plant shape is another element to consider. Cottage gardens generally showcase some billowing plants, which add lush softness; examples include summer phlox *(P. paniculata),* some kinds of asters, baby's breath, and shrubs such as lilacs. Plants with tall, narrow flower spikes, including delphiniums, foxgloves, and hollyhocks, make bold contrasts to lower and rounder plants. Plants that drape—over walls, trellises, and arbors—bring a cottage look to the garden; climbing roses and honeysuckle are classic examples. Add low-growing, spreading plants to soften the hard edges of paths, patios, and terraces. Sweet alyssum, pinks, lamb's ears, and violas all fit this role.

How you arrange plants of differing sizes also contributes to a cottage garden effect. In more formal gardens, plants are often set in tiers, with the shortest in front, medium-size in the middle, and tallest in the back. While you don't want to obscure plants from view completely, in a cottage garden you may occasionally bring a larger plant to the front—perhaps a fragrant shrub rose so that you can savor its scent more easily. Arranging irregularly shaped clumps or drifts of three or more of the same plant also helps give a casual cottage look and avoids the tyranny of tiers.

Spreading Self-Sowing Annuals and Biennials

The relaxed style of cottage gardens favors easy-to-grow annuals and biennials. Annuals complete their life cycle within a single growing season: the seed germinates, and the plant grows, blooms, sets seed, and dies. In contrast, biennials have a two-year life cycle. During the first year, biennials grow from seed to form a rosette of foliage; the following year, they bloom, set seed, and die. Many annuals and biennials obligingly self-sow, reappearing every spring with no effort on your part. Self-sowing annuals include calendula, poppy, love-in-a-mist, Johnny-jump-up, and sweet alyssum. Among the biennial self-sowers are two classic cottage garden plants: hollyhock and foxglove. If you want self-sowers to grow in new areas of your garden, you can give nature a hand by collecting and sowing some of the seeds yourself, rather than allowing them to self-sow randomly. Gather seed heads when they turn brown, taking them from healthy, vigorous plants. Pick the seed heads, and lay them on a paper-lined tray to dry. If the seed capsules are inclined to shatter, scattering the seeds, collect them in a paper bag. Once dry, crush the seedpods or capsules, if necessary, to release the seeds. Clean the seeds by placing them and the chaff in a shallow container; blow lightly to remove chaff and dust. You can plant the seeds immediately or store them in envelopes kept in a dry place and sow them in spring.

Growing a Rose on an Arch

Festooned with romantic flowers, climbing roses transform an arch, arbor, or pergola, bringing instant cottage garden charm. When planning such a feature, keep in mind that roses need well-drained soil at a sunny site. Select a variety that will grow to a height appropriate for your structure; some sorts reach only 7 feet, while others can grow as high as 30 feet.

1. Plant one rose at the foot of each post, about 15 inches from it, to allow room for the roots to develop. As the rose canes grow, guide them up and around the posts, separating them to encourage flowering shoots to develop along them. Tie the canes to the posts with bands of plastic tape, strips of cloth, or twine; don't use wire, which eventually constricts growth.

2. When the canes reach the tops of the posts, bend them over the structure. Train some stems along any diagonal braces as well. If the canes aren't too stiff, wrap them around the top of the arch; this makes the rose produce more flowering shoots. Tie the canes in place as needed during the growing season.

Making Use of Prunings

Twigs, branches, saplings, and vine cuttings from pruning jobs can all be put to good use in your cottage garden, where their rustic appearance fits right in.

Push small twigs or branches, about 1 to 2 feet long, into the soil near where you sow seeds of floppy annuals, such as bush-type sweet peas. Sticks this size are also useful for supporting perennials that tend to flop, such as asters. To edge flowerbeds, form overlapping hoops from longer, more flexible prunings.

Use stronger prunings to support larger plants, such as vining sweet peas, pole beans, and peas: for example, make a tepee from four 8-foot-long branches or saplings, lashed together at the top with twine. Put the tepee in place before sowing the seeds or setting out the plants.

Rustic trellises are fun to make from thicker pieces of wood. For the framework, look for fairly straight pieces, 1 to 1½ inches in diameter. If you have interesting twisted or branching pieces, use them to make diagonal and fan shapes within the framework; supple wood, such as freshly cut willow, can be used to form arches. Fasten the branches together with nails and wire.

Choosing a Picket Fence

Picket fences and cottage gardens (like this one designed by Kristen Horne) seem to go hand in hand. A picket fence gives a clear boundary to the garden, while leaving it open to public view. It also provides welcome support for a rambunctious assortment of tall and vining plants. The open structure lets air circulate well in the beds on either side, which is important for healthy plant growth.

A wide range of picket treatments and post tops is available. While classic pickets have simple pointed tops, the tops might also be rounded, arched, or cut into fancier shapes. Similarly, the posts can be square on top, beveled, or embellished with finials of various sorts. Generally the pickets are made of 1-by-3-inch boards spaced 2½ inches apart, but this can vary, too. In some fences, thicker 2-by-2-inch pickets are used; in others, the pickets are spaced more closely. While picket fences are often painted white, you may choose to match the color of your house, or leave the wood to weather naturally. Whichever design and color you favor, keep in mind that a simple style usually sets off a cottage garden most effectively.

Plants and Materials

Cottage gardens are an eclectic assortment of colorful, free-spirited plants—in other words, almost anything goes! Closely planted annuals, biennials, perennials, shrubs, roses, and vines, as well as edibles (see page 106), all contribute to the look of relaxed chaos. A few classic, longtime cottage garden favorites are described here. Except as noted, all grow in full sun to partial shade and require regular watering and fertilizing. Hardiness is noted in parentheses.

The swaying spires of delphiniums epitomize the English cottage garden. Shown here is the D. elatum *hybrid 'Purple Ruffles'.*

Aster

Old-fashioned favorites, New England aster, *A. novae-angliae,* and Michaelmas daisy, *A. novi-belgii* (both −30°F/−34°C), grow 4 to 5 feet tall and nearly as wide, with a soft, billowing form. Airy sprays of violet-blue flowers appear in fall. Many named selections are available, offering more compact plants and a wider color range, including white, pink, blue, and wine red.

Calendula (C. officinalis)

Also known as "pot marigold," because, in times past, both leaves and flower petals went into the cooking pot, this daisy-flowered annual is now treasured for the beauty it brings to the cool-season garden. Blossoms may be single, semidouble, or double, in orange, yellow, cream, and white; plant size varies from 1 to 2½ feet high and 1 to 1½ feet wide.

Delphinium (D. elatum hybrids)

With their 5- to 8-foot stems reaching skyward, packed with 2- to 3-inch-wide flowers, delphiniums provide a bold contrast to lower-growing, rounded plants. The most widely planted are the summer-blooming *D. elatum* hybrids (−20°F/−29°C), which include numerous named selections bearing flowers in pure blue, violet, pink, purple, white, and bicolors. They grow best in climates offering cool, mild summers; if grown in warmer regions, they need some shade from summer sun.

Foxglove (Digitalis purpurea)

A popular cottage garden biennial, foxglove (−20°F/−29°C) forms a clump of large tongue-shaped leaves in its first year. The next spring, a sturdy stem rises from the clump's center to about 6 feet, carrying tubular flowers shaped like the fingertips of a glove; blooms may be cream, white, rosy purple, or pink, all usually spotted purple on the inside. The 3-foot-tall Foxy strain, unlike the others, blooms in just 5 months from seed and can be grown as an annual. Plant foxgloves in light shade; in cool-summer regions, they also do well in full sun.

Hollyhock (Alcea rosea)

With their tall stems covered with single or double saucer-shaped flowers rising from a mounding clump of nearly round leaves, hollyhocks (−40°F/−40°C) are quintessential vertical accents for cottage gardens. Many named strains are available in a wide range of flower colors; they vary in height from 2½ to 8 feet. Though hollyhocks are biennial by nature, some have been bred to live for several years, and there are fast-growing annual strains.

Honeysuckle (Lonicera)

Woody, twining vines with, in these selections, fragrant flowers, honeysuckles are decorative additions to trellises and arbors. Goldflame honeysuckle, *L. × heckrottii* (−10°F/−23°C), grows to 15 feet high with lightly scented yellow and coral-pink flowers from spring until frost. Woodbine, *L. periclymenum* (−20°F/−29°C), twines to 20 feet. In summer and fall, its blossoms—purple on the outside, creamy white within—perfume the air. Both are evergreen where winters are mild, deciduous elsewhere.

Love-in-a-Mist (Nigella damascena)

This old-fashioned spring-blooming annual is a wispy, misty plant, 1½ to 2 feet tall, with threadlike leaf segments and blossoms backed by a ruff of filigree foliage. The flowers are followed by horned, paper-textured seed capsules that are decorative in their own right. Flowers come in blue, white, violet, and pink.

Pink *(Dianthus)*

Perennial pinks have been components of cottage gardens in England and elsewhere for centuries, offering cheerful flowers with a spicy fragrance of cloves. Cheddar pinks, *D. gratianopolitanus* (–40°F/–40°C), form a ground-hugging mat of blue-green leaves; round, fringed, pink, red, or bicolored flowers appear in summer on 6- to 10-inch stems. Cottage or grass pinks, *D. plumarius* (–40°F/ –40°C), grow into a loose mat of gray-green foliage, topped in summer by 10- to 18-inch stems bearing dark-centered flowers in rose, pink, or white.

Summer Phlox *(P. paniculata)*

Blooming in midsummer, perennial summer or border phlox (–30°F/–34°C) carries its fragrant flowers in large, dome-shaped clusters up to 8 inches across on 2- to 4-foot-tall plants. Flower colors include white and shades of lavender, pink, rose, red, and near-orange, some with a contrasting eye. Look for cultivars somewhat resistant to powdery mildew, a frequent problem on summer phlox; these include 'Bright Eyes', pink with a red eye, and white-flowered 'David'.

Sweet Pea *(Lathyrus odoratus)*

One of the best-known garden flowers, sweet peas are annuals that offer a delightful combination of beauty, color, and fragrance. Flowers are borne in long-stemmed clusters in white, blue, purple, violet, red, pink, and various bicolors. Vining types of sweet peas climb to 5 feet or higher. There are also bushy strains, ranging from a mere 4 inches to 3 feet high. Provide support for vining sweet peas and the taller bushy sorts as well (see page 109).

Viola

The simple country charms of Johnny-jump-ups, violas, and pansies have made these spring-blooming annuals welcome in cottage gardens for generations. Johnny-jump-ups *(V. tricolor)* grow about 1 foot high, with small purple-and-yellow blossoms; they self-sow freely. Reaching 8 inches high, violas *(V. cornuta)* bear 1- to 2-inch flowers in a wide range of colors, some with "whisker pattern" veins on the petals. Pansies *(V. × wittrockiana)* have showier flowers, to 4 inches across, in a huge variety of colors and color combinations on 1-foot-tall plants.

Cottage Garden Benches

As a finishing touch, add a comfortable wooden bench to your cottage garden. (This garden was designed by Betty Lou Davis.) Paint the bench to match your house or picket fence, or choose one made of teak or other tropical hardwood for its resistance to insects and rot as well as its beauty and strength. To avoid depleting tropical forests, look for Forest Stewardship Council (FSC) certification—it means that imported woods have been sustainably harvested. Either let a wooden bench weather to a natural gray or treat it with a sealer to preserve the new look. When buying a bench, check that all joints are strong and well made.

Heirloom Flower Varieties

Old-fashioned flower varieties, such as these sweet peas, are especially suited to cottage gardens. Most have a soft, relaxed look, with small or single blossoms; in comparison, modern hybrids tend to be stiff, with large flowers in strident colors. For mail-order seeds try Baker Creek Heirloom Seeds, www.rareseeds.com; Renee's Garden, www.reneesgarden.com; and Select Seeds Antique Flowers, www.selectseeds.com.

Climbing Rose

Climbing roses are a cottage garden tradition, whether planted to drape over the front door, festoon an arbor, or decorate a tripod or pillar. Though they vary in height from 7 feet to more than 30 feet, all climbing roses produce long, strong canes that will grow upright, provided you train and tie them (see page 108). Besides height differences, climbing roses vary in bloom season (some bloom only in spring; repeat-bloomers give several waves of flowers from spring until frost), fragrance, and, of course, flower size, shape, and color. Hardiness varies, too. Many need some protection where winter temperatures regularly dip to 10°F/–12°C or below.

A few favorite climbers that flower throughout the season are red-flowered 'Dortmund' (to 12 feet high; taller in warm climates), white 'Climbing Iceberg' (to 15 feet), and 'New Dawn', with fragrant, silvery pink flowers (to 15 feet). In very cold regions (where temperatures drop below –30°F/–34°C), look for the extra-hardy Canadian Explorer roses, such as 'William Baffin', which has large clusters of slightly fragrant carmine-pink blossoms on a plant that climbs to about 12 feet.

Sanctuary and Feng Shui Gardens

A sanctuary or feng shui garden quiets the mind while rousing the senses. It has a place of rest, a comfortable and lovely seat in a sheltered, harmonious, beautifully maintained space. All around it are sensory pleasures, such as birdsong, bells, whispering leaves, dewy buds, fragrant flowers, and a view of trees, water, or sky. For perfect tranquillity, the garden also has a sense of time immemorial and everything being right in the world.

Design, left: Davis Dalbok.

INDOORS, A FIREPLACE makes a beautiful focal point for a room; it draws people together into an atmosphere of comfort and reverie. An outdoor fireplace works the same way and is even more magical: to stare into the flames while sitting under the stars, with the evening shadows at the edge of the firelight, seems to satisfy an ancient longing. In a small space, consider a fire pit (see page 122); choose chairs that are comfortable and the right height for gazing into the embers.

Straight paths disperse ch'i (the earth's energies) too quickly, say feng shui practitioners, and are best avoided. If you have a straight path, give it the appearance of curves by placing plants alongside that spill over the edges.

A SIMPLE OUTDOOR resting place, this daybed is tucked against a long-flowering wall of lavatera in Jeffrey Bale's backyard in Portland, Oregon. Bale constructed the frame from poles and sturdy sticks and hung temple bells on it. Bells, wind chimes (see page 125), and fountains (see page 123) produce pretty sounds that change as a breeze picks up and falls away; they can mask street or neighborhood noise that might threaten a sense of sanctuary.

If you have any of the following already in your garden, use it as a starting point for a sanctuary or feng shui garden:

- comfortable seat
- sheltered area
- fragrant plants
- ancient-looking carvings, columns, figures
- venerable tree
- water feature
- sky view

A sanctuary or feng shui garden is an excellent choice for a quiet porch or patio, an area with a water feature, or a place with a sunrise or sunset view.

READING A POEM, psalm, or invocation can bring as much pleasure as fragrant blossoms or an inspiring view. This meditative labyrinth of text begins (at the outer edge) "If the Earth were only a few feet in diameter and floating a few feet above a field somewhere, people would come from everywhere to marvel at it." For information on creating a labyrinth to walk through, see page 122.

THIS FENG SHUI GARDEN was designed by Pamela Woods to be in complete harmony with nature. It is open in the center and the path is curved so that ch'i flows well through the garden. It has a balance of light and shade, warm colors and cool colors, hard boulders and gently flowing water. All five elements—water, fire (represented by red flowers), wood, metal, and earth (represented by yellow flowers)—through which ch'i manifests itself are present. And the garden has no clutter or ailing plants, factors said to negatively affect ch'i.

A SOAK IN an outdoor bathtub filled with steaming hot water would be a great way to start the day, thought California designers and homeowners Anne-Marie and Jeff Allen. They gave an old tub a coat of green enamel, set it on a large stone slab, and had the necessary plumbing installed. A purchased screen and plantings of New Zealand flax, golden currant, and abutilon provide privacy. Gardenia, jasmine, sarcococca, and sweet olive fill the air with fragrance.

FENG SHUI practitioners are careful with color, especially vibrant colors like red, which can feel too strong. Green promotes a sense of tranquillity. Blue is soothing. Purple is passionate and associated with dreaming, creativity, and spiritual practice.

Too much enclosure feels oppressive. Transform a very closed space by opening a view through a boundary fence or hedge. For more ideas on energizing space (activating ch'i), see page 120.

A SANCTUARY REQUIRES a strong sense of shelter, which you can achieve in several ways. Consider creating a secluded walk within a pergola *(left)* or placing a bench against a house wall and under a tree *(above)* or beneath a garden umbrella with tall plants surrounding it, as Tom and Stephanie Feeney did in their garden *(below)*. Look for a place where there's a special atmosphere, because of sunlight swimming through leaves or a view out under tree blossoms—or just because it's at the far edge of the garden and on the way there you can pick a handful of fresh peas or figs. For more ideas on creating a private space for your place of refuge, see page 121. Design, left: Heronswood Nursery.

THIS ROOFED SHELTER set cozily almost into the hedge provides sanctuary during inclement weather. You might stay during a rain shower to watch the raindrops splash in the pond and roll into the cupped water lily pads. To maintain an atmosphere of beauty, keep water clean and fresh looking.

Clear views and free movement are important in feng shui gardens. Tall hedges around the house, windows overgrown with vines, an entrance garden with spiky plants and a profusion of pots on the doorstep: these represent restrictions and are avoided.

TREES ARE SACRED in many ancient cultures. They are believed to hold spirits or the soul. They connect a garden to the mysterious life deep in the soil, the underworld, and also to the sky, heaven. Plant one special long-lived tree in a small garden; keep it a little away from the house, or it will block the flow of ch'i, according to feng shui experts. If space permits, consider a grove of trees, and make a clearing among them for an especially magical refuge. Place boulders there for seats; plant blue or purple flowers for a dreamy, meditative atmosphere. Design: Roger Warner.

Here are some ways to settle your sanctuary or feng shui garden alongside a part of your garden with a different theme. For more information, see pages 4–13.

Choose fragrant plants or plants with excellent sensory qualities. If the area next to your sanctuary or feng shui garden is a Mediterranean or cottage garden, lavenders and fragrant roses work well to link them. Ornamental grasses can link a sanctuary or feng shui garden to a natural one; red flowers, which generate a feeling of energy, make an effective transition to a tropical garden. Use decorative piles of stone or meditation objects to link a sanctuary or feng shui garden to a Japanese garden or an area with a personal, eccentric theme.

TO PROTECT his roof garden from strong breezes—wind destroys the calm of a sanctuary and sends people quickly back indoors—Sid Dickens built a windbreak of potted trees and vines. Note how invitingly comfortable the chaise looks; a view of it is sufficient to draw you outdoors. The "tiled" floor was sponge-painted by artist Wade King. Real tile would have been too heavy for the roof to bear.

A SMALL FIGURINE or stone head set in a quiet, sheltered place can become a spiritual heart of the garden. You might find yourself or your children taking little treasures there. Such a place could be a shrine with religious objects if you like, or simply a place to remember someone you love, planted with flowers that conjure memories. For more ideas on creating simple rituals, see page 121.

Applying the Concept of Ch'i to Your Garden

The notion of ch'i is central to the ancient Chinese philosophy and practice of feng shui. Ch'i is an invisible force or energy that infuses the entire universe. It is believed to circulate through the environment, including our homes and gardens, and to be essential to our well-being, happiness, and health. The principles of feng shui are intended to attract and activate the beneficial qualities of ch'i through placement of buildings, furniture, paths, plants, and other objects.

While feng shui has been interpreted in a number of ways, its basic ideas can be useful in garden design, especially in creating peaceful sanctuaries. Feng shui gardens aim for simplicity, with a natural, unforced look. Clutter is banished, as are dead or unhealthy plants, because they are said to make ch'i stale and upset the balance and harmony of the garden. Rather than tracing a straight line, paths are laid out to meander gently, so that beneficial ch'i does not flow quickly away from the garden. Fragrant flowers, evergreen shrubs and trees, and well-placed arbors are used to activate ch'i and improve its flow or circulation.

Light, whether reflected from a snow-covered glass ball, a still body of water, or a mirror, is thought to bring ch'i to the garden. You can also invite light and new views into the garden by making circular windows in solid walls or fences.

The movement of leaves stirring in the breeze, bamboo and grass stems brushing against one another, and water flowing down a gentle stream represent the natural flow of ch'i.

Plants with red leaves or flowers are often included in the feng shui garden to activate ch'i. This beneficial color represents life, happiness, good fortune, and prosperity.

Soft sounds of water trickling from a bamboo spout, birdsong, insects, and wind chimes hung at the corners of the house all help activate ch'i.

Creating a Private Space

Make a part of your garden into a peaceful retreat or sanctuary where you can relax, meditate, practice yoga, or simply take a nap. To separate this private space from the house and its everyday concerns, you don't necessarily need lots of space. In a small garden, create an oasis at one end of a patio or deck. In a larger garden your sanctuary might be an arbor or gazebo in a far corner or a tree house hidden high in an old oak.

You may screen at least part of the space to achieve a sense of shelter and privacy, but take care not to make it too closed in and dark. Walls or fences create immediate privacy. They can be solid or partially open to views beyond. Strings of beads or roll-up screens of bamboo or canvas offer further privacy options, as do big pots placed in a semicircle around a bench. Though slower to develop, large shrubs and clipped hedges make walls of green, many with seasonal blossoms.

An overhead canopy adds immeasurably to the sense of shelter, especially if there are tall buildings nearby. A tree with wide-spreading branches provides a leafy shelter.

Or build an arbor over which vines can scramble, forming a natural roof. An umbrella creates an instant "ceiling."

Add a bench or chair to your retreat, complete with comfortable cushions. Many people feel more secure with something, such as a wall or tree, against their backs when seated. Choose a location with a wonderful view of the garden. A small table, to hold a cup of tea, a candle, or a vase of flowers, is welcome, too. Other furnishings might include a water basin or small fountain. A birdbath and feeder make your space a sanctuary for birds as well as people.

Creating Simple Rituals

Small ceremonies and symbolic acts have a calming effect, which seems intensified when practiced in the garden. For instance, floating a few fresh flowers every morning in a water bowl or birdbath allows you to begin the day in a peaceful setting, while observing the delicate beauty of the blossoms. You might create a niche adorned with items of special importance in your life, such as drawings or photos, gifts from family and friends, beautiful seedpods or stones, small sculptures, or crystals; re-arranging the mementos periodically keeps you in touch with their meaning. Try making a cairn—a pile of small, flat pebbles, perhaps collected at the seashore or on a riverside camping trip. Sand painting is another calming, quiet activity. Place 1 or 2 inches of sand in a box or tray, and use a twig or small piece of driftwood to draw objects, designs, or symbols in the sand.

Other sorts of garden rituals include annual celebrations of the first apple blossoms of spring, the harvest season, or the brilliant colors of autumn leaves. The garden is also a perfect setting for a yearly May Day observance or a summer solstice camp-out under the stars.

Creating a Labyrinth

Labyrinths have been made in churches, public places, and gardens since ancient times. They often symbolize the path of life's journey. (This one was designed by Mark and Kelly Sanchez for their garden, designed by Peter Hanson.)

You might use a labyrinth as a meditation tool or simply for relaxation or even as a place that's fun for children to explore. The design may be a simple spiral or a more complex series of interlocking circles. For most people, labyrinths are the same as mazes, but some authorities make a distinction: labyrinths have a clearly defined way in and out; mazes have twists and turns and blind alleys, presenting a puzzle to be solved.

You can create a garden labyrinth out of many sorts of materials, including stones, bricks, concrete, tiles, or sticks arranged to outline a simple pathway. Other possibilities include mowing a pattern in tall grass or planting turf to form a design.

Before laying out a labyrinth, measure the space, and draw potential designs to scale on graph paper. This allows you to move the elements around until you have created a design that fits your space and ideas.

Adding a Fire Pit or Outdoor Fireplace

People never tire of staring into the mysterious, flickering flames of a campfire. Making a fire pit brings the magic of fire to your backyard, casting its spell on all within its glow. Whether you place your fire pit on a civilized terrace or on plain soil like a real campfire, be sure to keep it away from overhanging trees.

Clear all vegetation, such as grass, pine needles, and leaves, within 5 or 6 feet of the fire ring. Then dig a shallow pit, removing any roots. Surround the pit with rocks or bricks. When using the fire pit, always have a bucket of water or a hose nearby, and never leave the fire unattended. To put the fire out, douse it with water, and rake out the coals to make sure they are dead.

In areas where open-air fires are banned, you can create a similar effect with a chimenea. Originally made of clay, these freestanding portable fireplaces are now constructed of various metals, so that they are sturdier; today's versions are equipped with spark arresters and small-mesh screens for safety. Lower-profile freestanding metal units that burn propane or natural gas are also sold.

Making a Container Fountain

Falling water brings motion and life to a garden, deck, or private sanctuary. It also brings wonderful sound, a peaceful note that can mask noises from outside the garden.

You can make a fountain in a container quickly and easily. For the container, choose a glazed or unglazed ceramic pot without a drainage hole. (If your pot has a hole, plug it with a cork, and cover the area with a layer of epoxy.) Seal an unglazed container with a latex sealer manufactured for terracotta; let the sealer dry as directed on the label.

Small submersible pumps with fountainhead attachments are available at garden centers and nurseries that offer pond supplies; some are solar powered. If you place the fountainhead nozzle just below the water, it makes a low-bubbling fountain like a spring; placed above the water it makes a jet or fancy spray pattern, depending on

the nozzle type. Arranging the nozzle so that the water flows over and around stones gives yet another effect. The pump outlet can also be threaded through a hole drilled in a rock or other object, such as a ceramic frog or even a teapot (the hole is drilled in the bottom). Either choose a simple design, featuring only a container and water, or embellish the container with stones, shells, or glass balls.

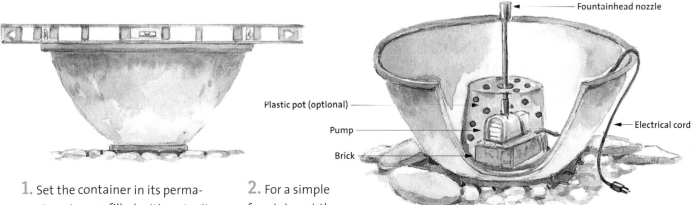

Fountainhead nozzle

Plastic pot (optional)

Pump

Brick

Electrical cord

1. Set the container in its permanent spot: once filled with water it will be too heavy to move. Choose a location out of the wind, so that water will not be blown around, and near a properly installed GFI outlet. Bury the electrical cord for the pump if it could trip someone; first push it through 1-inch PVC pipe if there is any danger a shovel could cut it. Rinse the pot and any stones you plan to use. With a carpenter's level, check that the pot is level.

2. For a simple fountain, set the pump on clean bricks in the bottom of the container, and lead the cord over the side; conceal the cord with plants. If you add pebbles or stones to your container fountain, protect the pump from them with an upturned plastic pot; drill or punch holes in the pot to allow water to circulate and the cord to exit. Push the fountainhead attachment through a hole in the plastic pot.

3. Fill the container with water, and plug in the pump. Adjust the water flow and arrangement of stones or other elements. Be sure to keep the container filled with water; if the water level becomes too low, the pump will fail.

Plants and Materials

Plants selected for feng shui and sanctuary gardens often have a symbolic meaning to the gardener. They may recall special friends or relatives or notable events. Certain plants may evoke childhood memories, for example of playing in a beloved grandmother's garden. Shrubs and vines might be chosen to help create or enhance a private space by screening an area. Fragrant plants or those with brightly colored flowers or soft textures stimulate the senses, making a sanctuary garden even more attractive and enjoyable. Except as noted, the plants described here grow best in full sun to partial shade and in well-drained soil; they need regular watering and fertilizing. Hardiness is noted in parentheses.

Chocolate Cosmos
(C. atrosanguineus)

With deep brownish red flowers that exude a strong perfume of chocolate, this perennial cosmos (0°F/−18°C) adds a delicious note to the late-summer garden. The 2½-foot-tall stems with coarsely cut leaves grow from a tuberous root. Because chocolate cosmos begins to grow later in spring than most other perennials, be sure to mark the plant's location. Mulch to protect the tubers in winter, or, in colder climates, dig them out of the ground, and store them (see page 95).

Chrysanthemum (C. × morifolium)

Sometimes referred to as "florists' chrysanthemums" (−20°F/−29°C), these hybrids are favorite perennials for the fall garden, available in many flower forms, colors, and plant sizes. In China, where chrysanthemums have been grown for centuries, they are thought to bring happiness into the home and are associated with a life of relaxation. Set out plants in spring; pinch back the growing tips frequently to encourage bushy growth with lots of blossoms.

Crocosmia

Featuring sword-shaped leaves, crocosmia (−10°F/−23°C) has branched stems of bright flowers that appear in summer. Hybrid forms offer interesting variations on the familiar, orange-flowered montbretia (C. × crocosmiiflora). 'Lucifer', which grows a robust 4 feet high, has bright red blooms. The 2-foot-tall 'Emily McKenzie' is also showy, bearing deep orange blossoms with red throats.

Lamb's Ears (Stachys byzantina)

With thick, soft, furry leaves that beg to be petted, lamb's ears (−30°F/−34°C) are classic foreground plants for the border. The basic species forms a spreading mat of 4- to 6-inch-long leaves; upright 1- to 1½-foot flower stems rise in spring, bearing whorls of small blossoms. 'Big Ears', which boasts leaves about twice as large, is a shy bloomer but makes an excellent ground cover for a small area.

Lilac (Syringa vulgaris)

A favorite from grandmother's garden, lilacs fill the air in spring with their legendary fragrance. These deciduous shrubs (−40°F/−40°C) can reach 20 feet high with nearly equal spread. The leaves are medium green, broadly oval in shape, with a pointed tip. Flowers in lavender, white, pink, or magenta are produced in clusters up to 10 inches long. Most kinds do best in regions with subfreezing winter temperatures; in warmer areas look for the Descanso Hybrids, developed to perform with only a little winter chill.

Mexican Orange (Choisya ternata)

A handsome, 6- to 8-foot-tall evergreen plant for an informal hedge or screen, Mexican orange (15°F/−9°C) produces clusters of fragrant, orange-blossom-like flowers in early spring, often continuing intermittently through summer. The lustrous dark green leaves are divided into fans of three leaflets up to 3 inches long.

Mock Orange (Philadelphus)

Beautiful white flowers with the delightful fragrance of orange blos-

A sturdy trellis of weathered wood is ideal for creating a private sanctuary, especially when embellished with a cloud of white flowers on a luxuriant clematis vine.

Clematis

In addition to providing a leafy screen for quiet retreats, clematis vines offer showy flowers followed by interesting fluffy seedheads. Most are deciduous. The large-flowered hybrid clematises (−20°F/−29°C) are popular; growing about 10 feet high, they bloom in spring and summer. These include 'Niobe', which has rich, dark red blossoms; purple *C. × jackmanii*; and white 'Henryi'. Golden clematis, *C. tangutica* (−20°F/−29°C), grows 15 feet high. Its bright yellow, nodding, lantern-shaped blossoms appear from midsummer to fall; the silvery seed clusters are especially handsome. The evergreen clematis species, *C. armandii* (10°F/−12°C), grows quickly to as high as 35 feet, with fragrant white flowers in spring. Provide a cool area for the roots of a clematis by adding mulch, placing a large rock over the root area, or planting in the shade of nearby shrubs.

soms appear in late spring on these vigorous deciduous shrubs. Many popular varieties are sold under the name *P. × virginalis* (most −20°F/−29°C), including 'Natchez' and 'Virginal'; both reach 8 feet high and wide. Double-flowered 'Enchantment' grows 6 feet tall and wide. Extra-hardy 8-foot-tall 'Minnesota Snowflake' (−30°F/−34°C) also has double flowers.

Nicotiana

With fragrant flowers that, in most varieties, open toward evening (and on cloudy days), annual nicotianas invite people to enjoy the garden at night. The wild species, *N. alata,* grows to 4 feet high, with slightly sticky leaves and stems, bearing white flowers. Many hybrids have been derived from it; some open in daytime and have pink or red flowers, but not all produce fragrant flowers. For guaranteed fragrance, plant white-flowered, 3-foot-tall 'Grandiflora'.

Peony (Paeonia)

Offering sumptuous, fragrant blossoms on handsome plants, herbaceous peonies (−40°F/−40°C) send up new shoots from bare earth in early spring, and then develop into bushy plants 2 to 4 feet high and wide. In mid to late spring, round buds open into satiny blossoms up to 10 inches across.

Flowers may be single, semidouble, or double; colors include red, pink, cream, and white. The handsome segmented leaves decorate the garden throughout the growing season.

Wintersweet (Chimonanthus praecox)

The small, translucent, pale yellow, spicy-scented flowers of wintersweet (−10°F/−23°C) do indeed appear in winter—or, in very cold areas, in early spring. They bloom on leafless branches, lasting for a month or more, if not hit by frost. This deciduous shrub grows slowly to 15 feet high and 8 feet wide. Find a location where the winter fragrance can be enjoyed, perhaps along an entrance path or beneath a bedroom window.

Wisteria

A twining, deciduous, woody vine of great size, bearing exceptionally beautiful flowers, wisteria is a good choice to cover a sturdy arbor. The bright green leaves are divided into many leaflets. Fragrant flowers appear in large clusters in blue, white, or pink. Japanese wisteria, *W. floribunda* (−20°F/−29°C), produces its 18-inch-long clusters of flowers during leafout, while Chinese wisteria, *W. sinensis* (−10°F/−23°C), blooms before the leaves expand; its flower clusters are about 12 inches long.

Candles, Lanterns, and Torches

The soft, flickering light cast by candles and oil-burning lamps brings a romantic glow to the nighttime garden. Light a wall with votive candles placed in terra-cotta pots. Use paper-bag luminaries to line a pathway: put a few inches of sand and a votive candle in the bottom of each bag. Hurricane lanterns made of glass, metal, or terra-cotta protect candle flames from wind; some types burn lamp oil. Lanterns mounted on long stakes make torches.

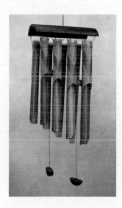

Wind Chimes

Set in motion by the slightest breeze, wind chimes and bells bring gentle melodies to your garden. You can select from a huge range of styles in many materials, including ceramic, metal, bamboo, and glass. Different styles make different sounds, from soft tinkles to solid gongs to precision-tuned chords. Test chimes before you buy, to be sure you like their sound. Once you install them, check that your neighbors like the sound, too. Other ways to introduce motion created by wind include wind streamers, mobiles, and wind sculptures.

Credits

Photography Credits

Paul Bousquet: 77 top

Marion Brenner: 2, 3 center top, 4, 11 bottom left, 15 bottom right, 17 bottom left, 25 top right, 41 top right, 62 top right, 70, 71 bottom left, 72 bottom left, 73 top, 76 top right, 118 bottom, 119 bottom

Karen Bussolini: 71 bottom right, 99 top right, bottom left, 120 bottom left

Ann Cecil: 89 top

Jack Chandler: 19 bottom right

Van Chaplin: 73 bottom

Glenn Christiansen: 55 bottom

Connie Coleman: 15 top right, 21 left

Claire Curran: 13 top right

Robin B. Cushman: 43 top left, 49 top left

Arnaud Descat/M.A.P.: 29 bottom left

Andrew Drake: 76 top left, 97 top

Roger Foley: 3 center bottom, 19 bottom left, 28, 34 top right, 39 top right, 42, 44 bottom right, 45 top, 63 left, 84, 86 top, 87 left, 88 top left, 90 top left, 98, 101 bottom, 111 top

Fiona Gilsenan: 36 top left

John Glover: 6 left, 7, 13 left, 27 top, 76 bottom right, 77 bottom, 82, 99 bottom right, 110, 113 top right, bottom right, 115 (2), 116 bottom left, 118 top left, 120 bottom right, 121 right, 125 top

Steven Gunther: 3 top, 11 bottom right, 14, 16 top left, 20 top left, 57 bottom right, 60 top left, bottom, 61 top, 94 top right, center left, center right, bottom, 114 top

Harry Haralambou: 44 top

Pamela Harper: 103 right

Jerry Harpur: 6 right, 9 bottom left, 15 bottom left, 17 right, 18 bottom, 21 right, 26, 31 bottom right, 34 bottom right, 47 (2), 64 top left, 102 right, 105 top left, bottom left

Marcus Harpur: 46 top left, 49 bottom left

Lynne Harrison: 13 bottom, 124

Sunniva Harte/The Garden Picture Library: 117 top right

Philip Harvey: 27 bottom, 41 bottom right

Saxon Holt: 33 top, 62 top left, 71 top right, 75 top left, 116 top

Michael Jensen: 19 top

Dency Kane: 29 top left, bottom right, 30 top, bottom right, 32 top right, 33 bottom, 34 bottom left, 45 bottom, 104 top left

Jacqueline Koch: 9 top left

Janet Loughrey: 31 top, 57 top right, 58 bottom right, 83 top, 105 right, 113 top left

Allan Mandell: 5, 46 right, 48 bottom, 78 top left, 91 top, 114 bottom right

Charles Mann: 11 top, 43 top right, 46 bottom left, 56, 57 bottom left

Sylvia Martin: 97 bottom

David McDonald/Photo Garden, Inc.: 51 top right

Sharron Milstein/Spindrift Photographics: 55 top

Yann Monel/M.A.P.: 59 bottom right

Terrence Moore: 94 top left

Clive Nichols/G.P.L.: 59 top

C. Nichols /M.A.P.: 68, 71 top left, 74 bottom left, 93 top right

Jerry Pavia: 20 bottom left, 22 top left, 32 bottom right, 62 bottom right, 85 bottom left, 103 top left

Norman A. Plate: 1, 60 top right, 63 right, 75 bottom, 83 bottom, 91 bottom

Matthew Plut: 16 bottom, 17 top left, 29 top right, 30 bottom left, 32 top left, 35 top left, 81 top right, 89 bottom right

Susan A. Roth: 40 top right, 43 bottom left, 67 top right, 69, 72 top left, 75 top right, 85 top left, top right, bottom right, 86 bottom left, 87 top right, bottom right, 88 top right, 90 top right, bottom right, 96, 99 top left, 100 (3), 101 top, 102 top left, 104 right, 109 top right, 111 bottom, 113 bottom left, 120 top right, center

Christina Schmidhofer: 3 bottom, 9 right, 15 top left, 88 bottom, 112

SPC Photo Collection: 102 bottom left

Thomas J. Story: 58 top, 122 top left, 125 bottom

Martin Tessler: 20 top right, 119 top

Michael S. Thompson: 48 top left

Mark Turner: 117 bottom

Craig Tuttle: 43 bottom right

Deidra Walpole: 52 top left, 74 right

judywhite/GardenPhotos.com: 18 top left, 35 bottom right, 57 top left, 59 bottom left, 61 bottom right, 72 top right, 106 top left, 117 top left

Ben Woolsey: 54

Acknowledgments

Thanks to Phil Edinger, Tom Chakas of Rebar Trees, Jana Olson Drobinsky, and Christina Jantzen Feng Shui Interior Design for providing information used in some of the projects in this book. Thanks to Kelly and Mark Sanchez for allowing us to photograph their labyrinth in Santa Cruz, California.

Plant Index

Pages listed in *italics* include photographs.

Subject Index

Pages listed in *italics* include photographs.